MAKING
MINIATURE GARDENS

MAKING
MINIATURE GARDENS

FREIDA GRAY

GUILD OF MASTER CRAFTSMAN PUBLICATIONS LTD

First published 1999 by
Guild of Master Craftsman Publications Ltd,
166 High Street, Lewes, East Sussex, BN7 1XU

Photographs on pages 9, 10, 11, 13 (left), 14, 15 (bottom), 16, 19, 24, 125, 146 (top) by Freida Gray
All other photographs by Anthony Bailey
Line drawings on pages 37, 52 (middle), 85, 100, 104, 109, 110, 119, 120, 122–5, 128, 132, 136–9, 148, 170–6 by John Yates
All other line drawings by Freida Gray

ISBN 1 86108 058 1

Designed by Christopher Halls at Mind's Eye Design, Lewes

Cover design by Rob Wheele at Wheelhouse Design, Brighton

Set in Caslon and Futura Book

Colour reproduction by Job Color srl – Gorle (BG) – Italy

Printed by Sun Fung Offset Binding Co Ltd

CONTENTS

Preface   vi

PART 1: TECHNIQUES AND MATERIALS

 1   Miniature Gardens: An Introduction   2

 2   Scale and Measurement   6

 3   Materials   8

 4   Tools and Equipment   17

 5   Methods   23

 6   Simple Plants   29

 7   Basic Flower-Making Techniques   33

 8   Making Specific Flowers   39

PART 2: PROJECTS

Safety   59

 9   Trellis Arch   60

10   Walled Garden   74

11   Patio Garden   86

12   Pond and Rockery   102

13   Cottage Garden   112

14   Greenhouse Garden   130

15   Kitchen Garden   152

16   Window Boxes   168

17   Further Uses for Miniature Garden Ideas   179

Conversion Tables   183

Index   184

PREFACE

This book is intended for those new to the hobby of miniatures. There is, therefore, no assumption of any previous knowledge of the basic tools, equipment, materials, or techniques involved. Most of the projects can be accomplished with the minimum of equipment, the greatest requirement being patience.

Although intended to be complementary to dolls' houses, the projects are complete models in themselves, and can make a fascinating pastime and hobby on their own.

Gardens have played an important part in our lives for centuries. Many large country houses were sited to give the best vista, with the gardens as an integral part of the whole design and planned to enhance the house itself. Although the average collector's dolls' house is not on this grand scale, a garden can, nevertheless, serve the same purpose.

There are many books about making dolls' house furniture and furnishings, from the very simple to those requiring amazingly intricate and skilled craftsmanship. Yet it seems to me that the potential for outside features has been somewhat neglected, and I hope that this book will go some way towards remedying this.

The object of this book is to show you how, by buying as little as possible ready made, you can make flowers, plants, furniture, and garden settings. Using these ideas you can create your own unique garden dream and display it with pride, knowing that 'I made it my way'.

PART 1:
TECHNIQUES
AND MATERIALS

CHAPTER 1

MINIATURE GARDENS: AN INTRODUCTION

Making model gardens 1/12 the size of real gardens is a fascinating occupation. The essential ingredients of success are imagination, ingenuity, and patience – mostly the latter. Materials can vary from household bits and pieces to specially purchased items, and the equipment used can vary from the very simplest – craft knife and scissors – to the most sophisticated, so it can be as cheap or expensive a hobby as you make it.

Of course, you cannot actually grow plants 1/12 the size of the real thing. Bonsai trees would be the nearest in scale, but they are either extremely costly or take many years to grow, and I have yet to find a so-called miniature rose that is truly 1/12 scale. Even a fully open rose only ³/₄in (19.1mm) across would represent a true-size rose 9in (229mm) across! To be realistic for 1/12 scale, a fully open miniature rose would need to be ¹/₂in (12.7mm) across at most, on a plant little over 4in (102mm) high – equivalent to 6in (152mm) flowers on a 48in (1219mm) high bush. However, effective representations of various plants and flowers can be fashioned in 1/12 scale from all kinds of unlikely materials. At their most simple they can be made up from bits of dried grasses and flowers, which are either dried at home or bought from your local flower shop, garden centre, or supermarket. Flowers and plants can also be created from paper of various kinds, and such things as crochet cotton or embroidery thread. It's not difficult – just fiddly.

One of the main differences between creating a 1/12 scale garden and creating the real thing, apart from the size and the physical effort involved, is that you are not dependent on the weather and can have a beautiful garden in full bloom all the year round. What's more, there is no grass to cut and there are no weeds! You are in complete control of the size, shape, and content of your miniature masterpiece – but beware: it can become just as much of an obsession as the real thing!

Each period of history had its own style of garden layout, furniture, and outside ornamentation. You only have to visit a few of the many stately homes open to the public to see this, particularly where they have re-created gardens as they would have been when the property was originally built. The range of plants commonly available has also changed vastly over the years. Many plants and flowers we now take for granted were just not around in earlier days, and conversely, many which were common in days gone by are now almost forgotten. The projects in this book have not been designed with any specific period in mind, so if you want to re-create a particular period it would be best to check that the things you want to include are appropriate for the period.

Nowadays, it is possible to buy a ready-made 1/12 scale model of just about anything you can think of for a collector's dolls' house and garden. If you have a bottomless purse and want a quick result with the minimum of effort, then you can buy what takes your fancy. Unfortunately, many of us cannot afford to do this; in any case, I think that by doing so you miss out on the most interesting part of miniatures – which is creating the whole thing yourself.

The plans and details given are intended to enable you to make interesting and decorative miniature gardens as shown in the photographs, but the plans don't have to be followed exactly. Ideas and individual items can be adapted and incorporated into your own designs, to form part of a collection, or just to stand alone as an interesting talking point.

Perhaps you have a 1/12 scale house where you display your miniature furniture? Add a garden, patio, or even a few tubs, hanging baskets, or window boxes, and you add a whole new dimension of interest. Should your interest be more in 1/12 scale dolls, then you will have a wealth of ideas, in these projects, for creating a superb new setting in which to display your dolls; and they, in turn, will complement your miniature garden. After all, dolls shown off in a garden setting can be seen and appreciated more easily and clearly than inside a room.

A small miniature garden can give great pleasure to a housebound friend or relative, or to an elderly person living in a flat or home with no garden of their own, particularly one who has had to give up their garden for one reason or another. Maybe you don't have a garden and just like to dream about what sort of garden you would like. These projects are the things that dreams are made of, and you can make your dream come true in miniature.

Whatever purpose you use any of the ideas in these projects for, don't forget that the main aim is to enjoy it, so happy gardening – in 1/12 scale, of course.

CHAPTER 2

SCALE AND MEASUREMENT

WORKING TO SCALE

People who are not used to the idea sometimes have difficulty in understanding exactly what is meant by 'working to scale'. For those of you who don't know already, I will try to explain it. Those who already know all about it can skip the next bit.

Working to 1/12 scale means, quite simply, that the measurements of the original are divided by 12 to give the scale size. It is possible to make models to any scale you like – the principle is always the same. For a 1/24 scale model you divide the original measurements by 24 to get the scale size, for 1/16 scale you divide by 16, and so on. It doesn't matter, therefore, what units of measurement are used, so long as the *same* units are used to measure both the original and the model: be it inches, millimetres, or even lengths of a matchbox. It is a mistake to try to mix different units, as this inevitably leads to complications and problems of all sorts, and soon chaos ensues.

This is 1/12 scale: a scale begonia and a real penny, shown actual size.

MATERIAL SIZES

Problems can arise, even when working from a detailed, dimensioned drawing and using the same units of measurement. Sometimes materials are sold with an Imperial size given (often referred to as a 'nominal' size), when the accurate size is metric. These 'nominal' sizes are the nearest Imperial size available to the actual metric size, or vice versa. In other words, they are close but not exact equivalents, and this must be borne in mind. To be absolutely sure, check the actual measurements of the material you are using.

MODEL GARDEN DRAWINGS

Being of the older generation, I was brought up with Imperial measurements, and so I tend to think in feet and inches. I can certainly visualize something 15 inches long, but have to do mental mathematical gymnastics to turn this into 381 millimetres. Similarly, if something is said to be 280 millimetres I cannot visualize how big this is without mathematical contortions to convert it to about 11 inches – my fault, undoubtedly, but I know for a fact that I am not alone. Conversely, those of my children's generation, and younger, naturally visualize in metric and are not sure how big an inch is. No doubt some of you reading this book belong to one camp and some to the other.

My drawings in this book are, as far as possible, the actual size for the models and, because I think in Imperial, the dimensions are normally given first in inches and fractions of an inch. To get around the problem of variations in sizes of materials as discussed above, I sometimes opt for the simple way out and use 'width of material' or 'half width of material' instead of a specific dimension. This way it doesn't matter whether the material is ¼in wide or 6mm wide, because you use the width of the material itself as the measurement. I also adopt the engineering drawing method of stating 'to fit'. In other words, the size given is theoretically correct; but because of possible slight differences in material size, or conversions from one unit of measurement to another, the actual size may be slightly different. It may be a little bit more or a little bit less; you will have to cut it to fit.

For plants and flowers, however, it is not necessary to do more than have them approximately the right size and proportions.

METRIC EQUIVALENTS

It is common practice in this sort of book to give two sets of measurements: either the Imperial with a metric equivalent, or vice versa. Giving exact metric equivalents which can be measured satisfactorily is not easy. There are exactly 25.4 millimetres in one inch; therefore, to change inches into millimetres you multiply the number of inches by 25.4. The result gives you the number of millimetres, which often has two or more decimal places. This is impractical for model garden structures, so I have opted for the most part to give Imperial measurements with their metric equivalents rounded to the nearest whole millimetre, except when there are fractions of an inch, in which cases I have given the metric equivalent rounded to one decimal place and leave it to your discretion as to whether it is better to go to the nearest whole millimetre higher or lower. For products available only in metric sizes, such as MDF, the metric dimension is given first. I have included some conversion tables of these equivalents at the end of the book (page 183).

If you *must* work in metric from Imperial measurements, particularly if you want to make a model from a full-size item for which you only have Imperial measurements, then because of the rounding up or down of calculations, for anything but the simplest model an exact scale drawing should be made to ensure that the bits will actually fit together properly. The alternative is to avoid the mathematics, buy an Imperial ruler, and work in inches.

I hope I have made things a little clearer, and that you are not more confused now than you were before you started!

CHAPTER 3

MATERIALS

The materials I use for making model gardens can be divided into two categories: those used for making the garden layout, structures, and furniture, which I call 'general materials'; and those used for creating the miniature flowers and plants. Some materials can, of course, be used for both. The list of materials which follows is not intended to be exhaustive, merely to give you some idea of the materials which I use.

GENERAL MATERIALS

WOOD

Wood is needed to make some of the furniture and structures, such as seats and trelliswork, in a model garden. Various kinds of wood are available already cut into various small-sized strips; for example balsa, pine, obeche, and oak. There are also very thin model-making plywoods which can be cut easily with a craft knife. These can all be used for making furniture and structures in model gardens, although for the items shown in this book I have used balsa for ease and simplicity.

Balsa is a wood often used for making model aeroplanes because it is very light in weight, and easily cut with the simplest of tools. However, it has a very open grain, which means that it is not suitable for fine finishing, but is very useful to simulate rough-sawn and weathered exterior timber such as you might find in many garden structures.

The other woods mentioned are harder and much more difficult to cut accurately without the proper equipment, although they can give a far superior finish, which is more suitable for some garden furniture. Specialist dolls' house wood sections can, of course, be used in the miniature garden very readily, and also give a fine finish, but they do tend to work out quite expensive and are not usually necessary.

'DO-IT-YOURSELF' PRODUCTS

Many of the things intended for household use can be used in making model gardens. Examples are MDF (Medium Density Fibreboard) or plywood, either of which can be used for baseboards and are available from do-it-yourself shops. I use many other DIY products, as they are easily available and relatively cheap. Many of the things left over from other jobs can be used in a model garden, or leftovers from a model garden can be used up on other jobs around the house. These include various kinds of household filler, such as Polyfilla; sealants, such as clear silicone sealant; wood stains, such as those made by Colron; as well as adhesives, paints, and varnishes.

ADHESIVES

There are now so many different adhesives on the market that it can seem quite bewildering. They vary from general-purpose adhesives, such as UHU, to very specialist ones, such as cyanoacrylate 'superglues'. I have my favourites, such as Loctite rapid wood glue and Evo-Stik Resin W woodworking glue, particularly the fast-setting variety. Where there is a gap to fill, because things didn't quite go according to plan and I need a strong joint, I use the good old stand-by – the epoxy-resin adhesive Araldite.

For flower making, one of the most useful adhesives I have found is Aleene's 'Tacky' glue. This dries clear and is almost invisible, but stays a bit flexible. I also use various PVA wood glues for sticking some flower bits together when I want a firmer hold. This also dries clear but sets hard. I find both the Bison and Bostik ranges of adhesives are very good, particularly those intended for use with plastics of one kind or another. Where 'tacky' glue is referred to in the text, PVA-type glue is a suitable alternative.

No doubt you will find some brands of glues are more readily available in your locality than others, and also that some are more suited than others to your way of working. You probably have your favourites anyway, but when you find a range of adhesives you are happy with, then stick to them (no pun intended!).

A selection of adhesives suitable for miniature garden making.

PAINTS

Model paints, such as Humbrol, both the enamel and acrylic types, are very useful in model garden construction, as there is such a wide range of colours available in small pots, and they dry quickly. Brushes used with enamel-type model paints need the proper thinners to clean them effectively, but the acrylic types can be washed out of brushes with water, provided they have not been allowed to dry out.

I have also used colour-match or colour-tester pots of household emulsion (latex) paint and exterior masonry paints for such things as paving stones and brickwork. For these products brush cleaning should be carried out according to the manufacturer's instructions on the container.

For large areas, such as the stone walling in Chapter 10, I sometimes use Rowney System 3 acrylic paint, which is available from art shops or art departments in large stores. This comes in fairly large squeezy plastic bottles with a replaceable cap. A few basic colours allow me to mix any colour I want: yellow ochre, blue, red, green, brown, white, and black are adequate for most things in the garden. Fabric paints are now easily available and serve very well for many flower-making purposes, to colour either silk or dried flowers. Most of these can be cleaned out of brushes with water, but check the manufacturer's instructions.

Suitable paints range from ordinary household emulsion to specialist model-makers' paints, all available in conveniently small quantities.

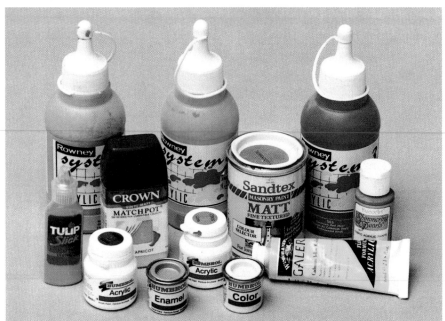

Although not really paints, another useful colouring medium is felt-tip pens. These are sold in many different shades nowadays and are a very useful quick, clean, and easy way of applying the small areas of colour needed to add detail to paper flowers and leaves.

VARNISH

The most useful type I have found is acrylic varnish. It comes in matt, satin, and gloss finish, either from the DIY shop, sold under various trade names, or from the model shop, made by firms like Humbrol. It is easy to apply, dries quickly, and your brushes can be cleaned easily in water immediately after use.

Humbrol also make a model varnish which is available in miniature spraycans. This makes getting an even coating on tiny bits much easier, and it can also be used as fixative (see page 14) to keep petals in place when making flowers.

BRUSHES

You will need brushes to apply the paint and varnish. These do not always need to be of the best artists' quality; the cheaper ones should be quite good enough for many purposes, with artists'-quality brushes reserved for very fine detail work. Painting large areas of styrofoam is not kind to paintbrushes, so keep your older ones for this job.

SPRAYING

An alternative method of applying paint, or indeed other colouring agents, is by spraying; and for some items this is the most practical solution, particularly for tiny bits of flower-making materials. Car spray paints are available in a very wide range of colours, but some have a cellulose base which is unpleasant and dangerous to breathe, and is also very flammable. Cleaning up after use is also a problem, and for cellulose-based paints can only be done successfully with proper cellulose thinners, which is equally dangerous and unpleasant.

Some paints are now available in 'ozone-friendly' aerosol sprays. The brand I use is made by Plasi-Kote: Odds n' Ends fast-dry spray enamel.

> **CAUTION:** It is essential when spraying that you avoid breathing the vapour, as it is very fine and can easily be breathed into your lungs along with tiny particles of paint. So always wear a mask to protect yourself, and only spray in a well ventilated area, away from naked flames and gas heaters, or better still, outside.

MODELLING MATERIALS

POLYMER CLAY

There are excellent modelling materials which are useful to the miniaturist. One of the most useful is a polymer clay material available under various trade names such as Fimo, Sculpey, and Formello. It handles very much like Plasticine, but sets hard when baked at a fairly low temperature for a short time in a domestic oven, preferably electric, but NOT a Microwave.

> *Cover a baking tray with baking parchment or tinfoil and place your models on this as you make them, spaced out so that they do not touch, then 'cook' them all at one go, according to the manufacturer's recommendations. For economy, this can be done when you have had the oven on for cooking something else. The temperature needed is fairly low (maximum 130°C), so when the oven is cooling down is a good time.*

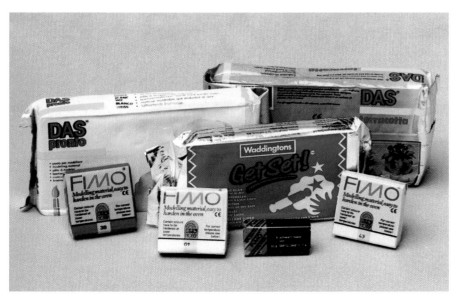

Polymer clay (foreground) and some well-known brands of air-drying clay.

Another useful modelling material is air-drying clay. This doesn't need cooking at all; it hardens by just being left to dry at room temperature. Couldn't be simpler! The length of time needed will vary, depending on the thickness of the clay and the size of the model – anything from a couple of hours to a couple of days. It is available under various trade names and in various colours – grey, white, and terracotta. The one I use mostly is Das, basically because it is easily available in the area where I live.

STYROFOAM

I find that the blocks of styrofoam sold for dry flower arrangements are indispensable. They are commonly referred to by one of the trade names, Oasis (in much the same way as some people refer to any vacuum cleaner as a Hoover no matter what make it is), but there are other brands, such as Dryfoam. I use them widely, for forming flowerbeds and for creating garden structures such as brick walls.

GRASS MATERIALS

To simulate grass you need to find some product which is easily available to you, with a colour and texture which suits your taste. I find some more realistic than others.

Green craft felt would seem an obvious option, but this is not very convincing, nor is it usually available in suitable shades of green. There is also a green flock velour self-adhesive material made by Fablon, which is quick and easy to use, but I find this too dark in colour to be realistic. Various shades of 'scatter' materials available for model railway layouts are another possibility, but are messy to use and not at all convincing.

The best grass material I have found is another one intended for railway layouts: a scenic grass mat, made from fibres stuck to a paper backing, and available in various shades of green. I find it easy to use, and consider that it gives a very good, realistic effect.

You don't have to use a special material – one of the most realistic effects I achieved some time ago was made by cutting up an old green velour curtain!

FLOWER AND PLANT MATERIALS

To simulate plants, flowers, bushes, etc. requires quite a bit of imagination and not a little patience! Before you can even begin, though, you will need a range of materials from which to make your plants and flowers. The next section lists some of the more common ones, but I suggest that you get into the habit of collecting anything which could possibly be used to represent a bush, plant, or flower, so that you will have as wide a choice as possible when it comes to 'planting' your garden.

Blocks of Oasis or Dryfoam are very useful as assembly aids when making paper flowers, and for storing completed flowers. I use a small block to hold a flower stem steady while I assemble the flower, and a larger block to store completed flowers. This allows the glue to dry without getting where it isn't wanted, and also keeps flowers safely together instead of sticking to your sleeves, or getting dropped on the floor and stood on.

GRASSES AND DRIED FLOWERS

Grass heads grow in many shapes and sizes and are easily collected and dried at home by simply standing them in a glass jar without water and leaving them to dry, or by hanging up bunches to dry in an airy place, after which they can be dyed or sprayed whatever colour is suitable.

There are many methods of preserving and drying flowers and plant material, but this is beyond the scope of this book; there are many books available on this subject if you want to dry small flowers yourself.

Alternatively, you can buy ready-dried flowers and other plant materials. A look in your local supermarket, or the nearest florist's, should give you a good idea of what is readily available commercially. My experience has been that many of these are too large for use with 1/12 scale unless they can be broken down into smaller bits.

One which I find almost indispensable, though, is sea lavender. This can be used in many different ways, and it is even possible to create an attractive garden scheme using this almost entirely (see Chapter 9, page 68). I also use the related plant statice, and to avoid any possible confusion I should point out here that when I refer to 'sea lavender' I mean *Limonium latifolium* (or *Statice latifolia*), while by 'statice' I mean *Limonium sinuatum* (or *Statice sinuata*).

Statice and sea lavender are available ready-coloured in a range of colours; the yellow flowers here are natural-coloured statice.

Many kinds of dried flower materials are suitable for our purposes.

BOUGHT SILK FLOWERS

Artificial flowers made from fabric of some kind are generally all referred to as 'silk' flowers, although they are unlikely to be made from silk. Bought ready made these can be expensive, and they are, once again, usually too large for 1/12 scale. I find that the most useful ones are those which have a flower head or spray form, which is made up of lots of small flowers. One stem of this type can provide flowers for a large part of a miniature garden. You may even have some silk flowers already, which can be recycled, by being cut up into smaller bits – leaves are particularly useful.

A selection of silk flower materials.

PAPER

The choice of paper may depend entirely on colour, or on the particular properties of the kind of paper, or a combination of both. Many of the flowers for my miniature gardens are made from acid-free tissue paper, which is available in many different colours. I also use paper table napkins, as there is now such a wide range of colours available, and the unused ones don't get wasted – they come in for their proper purpose when we have visitors.

Sometimes I use crepe paper, particularly where its stretchy qualities can be used to advantage, for flower shapes such as iris, for example. Unfortunately, for many things I find it is too coarse.

Various kinds of paper suitable for making flowers.

THREAD

Many kinds of flowers, such as chrysanthemums, dahlias, and daisy-like flowers, can be made from thread. I use various thicknesses of crochet cotton, which come in nice pastel colours, and stranded embroidery threads, which are available in an enormous range of shades.

FIXATIVES

For fixing paper, silk, and thread flowers in shape, and to keep petals where I want them, I use various products as fixatives. A very useful one, for a temporary hold, is hair fixative spray. The ones I use are the FX firm-hold fixing spray made by L'Oréal, or one of the Wella Shock Waves range. These don't dry too stiff, but hold the bits where I want them. There are many different brands available, from chemists' and supermarkets, with different holding properties – normal hold, firm hold, extra-firm hold – so experiment to see which ones suit you best. For a firmer fix, Humbrol mini-spray varnish is what I use, as mentioned above. Another useful one is also made by Humbrol: Krylon Crystal Clear, an acrylic spray which dries very quickly and gives a protective water-resistant coating.

Crochet and embroidery threads can be used to make chrysanthemums and daisy-type flowers.

Flower-making materials: fixatives, stem tape, and artificial stamens.

ARTIFICIAL STAMENS

Artificial stamens can be bought from shops selling cake-decorating or sugarcraft equipment, and from specialist suppliers of silk flower-making materials. They are available in different sizes and shapes, and in many colours, as well as white, which can be coloured with paint or food colouring to suit your flowers.

FLORISTS' STEM TAPE

Florists' stem tape, which is a sort of stretchy tape impregnated with tacky adhesive, is usually available in various greens or browns. This can be used to cover wire stems, and to hold a bunch of stems together to form a plant or a bush. Being both stretchy and sticky, it can be wound very tightly around a stem in a spiral fashion and pressed firmly to stay in place. Local florists, garden centres, or sugarcraft suppliers and suchlike should be able to supply this. This product used to be made with gutta-percha, a rubbery substance from certain Malayan trees, but this has inevitably been largely replaced nowadays by more modern synthetic materials.

If reindeer moss becomes dried out and is not pliable, dip it in water for a short time and then squeeze out the excess water.

REINDEER MOSS

Sometimes called 'lichen', sometimes labelled as 'reindeer moss' or 'decorative moss', this material is virtually indispensable for making miniature plants and bushes. It is a natural lichen which grows in very cold regions or on very high moors, and forms part of the main diet of reindeer – hence the name. Much of that sold in Britain comes from Norway.

Small bags are sold in a limited range of assorted colours for use on model railway layouts. Larger packets or boxes of a greater range of colours are often sold at large garden centres or chain stores for use with Vesutor air plants or for flower arrangement and decorating purposes.

Reindeer moss comes in a variety of colours.

WIRE

Florists' wire can be used as stems for flowers and plants, and it also serves to bind together bunches of materials for bushes and shrubs. Sometimes bare metal, and sometimes coated green, it is available in various sizes from most florists.

Another kind of covered wire which I use a lot is available from sugarcraft suppliers and cake-decorating shops. These paper-covered wires are generally thinner and more pliable than those used by the florist. They come in different sizes, or gauges: the smaller the number, the thicker the wire. I mostly use from 24 to 33 gauge.

Electrical wire is another unlikely but useful material for plant making, as is green plastic-coated garden wire.

Different gauges of wire are suitable for plant stems and many other uses.

HEDGEROW TWIGS

Hedgerow twigs can, of course, be used as the basis of a miniature shrub or tree. Strip off any leaves and allow the twigs to dry thoroughly before using them.

AQUARIUM PLANTS

Artificial aquarium greenery can often make convincing miniature plants 'off the shelf'.

A surprisingly useful source of materials for plants in a model garden is the local pet shop. Many artificial aquarium plants are now available with leaves of suitable shapes and small enough to be ideal for miniature plants and bushes.

MODEL RAILWAY LAYOUT MATERIALS

Railway layout materials.

Model shops and specialist model railway shops stock a wide variety of things which can be used in a model garden, apart from those already mentioned. What would be trees on a model railway layout serve well as shrubs or bushes in the much larger scale used for model gardens. There is a foam-flock scenic material from a firm called Heki, which can be put to good use for plants and bushes when stuck to covered wires; and some of the scatter materials from such companies as Peco are also useful for simulating soil, gravel, and suchlike.

ODDS AND ENDS

Save pictures from gardening magazines, seed and plant catalogues. Many full-colour advertisements can be turned into miniature packets of seeds, potting compost, etc. for garden accessories, and the magazines may also give you some ideas for your miniature garden.

Bottle tops of all shapes, sizes, and descriptions can be pressed into service (suitably modified) as plant containers and garden urns. Odds and ends of cake decorations, cotton reels, cardboard, small glass or plastic beads, buttons, and so on can all come in useful – the list is endless. Get into the habit of looking at things before you throw them out, and try to imagine if they could be used to simulate a flower, plant, pot, statue, or anything else you might want in your garden. Don't discard anything which could conceivably be used – in other words, develop what I call a 'scrap-box mentality'.

CHAPTER 4

Tools and Equipment

In listing some of the tools and equipment I use, I have assumed that you are new to the world of model making and miniatures, but I'm sure that those of you who are old hands at the game will forgive this assumption, and skip those bits about the tools and equipment that you already have. You may, however, still find some useful information about other bits and pieces I use.

WORKING AREA: GENERAL

It is important that, when working with sharp tools such as craft knives and razor saws, you don't try to work on a tray or board across your knees. Apart from making the job difficult, it is potentially dangerous. A firm table or bench is ideal, and, to protect not only the surface you are working on, but also the cutting edges of sharp tools, a purpose-made cutting mat is very useful. These can be bought from model shops, or by mail order from firms such as Hobby's.

WORKING AREA: FLOWER MAKING

For making the flowers themselves I prefer to use either a large tray with a ledge all round to keep bits from spreading too far, or an old tablecloth spread over my desk, or sometimes both.

As it can take a long time to make 1/12 scale flowers, it is important to sit somewhere where you are comfortable so that you don't get neck ache, or backache. If this means your favourite armchair, then make sure that you have a good light next to you (see 'Lighting' below). Working on a tray across your knees is fine, provided that you are not using anything more dangerous than paper and scissors – fine, that is, until you spill that cup of tea, and end up with a sort of paper soup on the tray, or the doorbell rings and you stand up quickly, leaving the floor looking like the aftermath of a wedding, strewn with a confetti of paper flower-making circles! So make sure there is a table handy to put the tray down on.

LIGHTING

Don't try to work with just ordinary room lighting; you will soon find this very trying on the eyes. A good desk light of the Anglepoise type, or one with a flexible stem that can be positioned right over your working area, is best.

Ordinary light bulbs distort colours, and fluorescent tubes are even worse, so avoid these if at all possible. What seemed like the right colour in electric light may look completely wrong in daylight. It is very disheartening when the previous evening's work turns out to have been a waste of time. I know – I've done it! There are now what are called 'daylight' bulbs, available from needlework and craft shops, which are intended to simulate natural daylight so far as colour values are concerned, and I find one of these very good for working with coloured papers, paints, and threads.

MAGNIFIERS

An important thing to bear in mind with magnifiers is that if they are left where the sun can shine on them it is possible for them to start a fire by focusing the heat from the sun's rays. (This used to be recommended to boy scouts for lighting camp fires!)

When working on small bits, there is no doubt that a magnifier, of one kind or another, is essential if you are to see exactly what you are doing, without straining your eyes or cutting your fingers. There are many fairly cheap but useful magnifiers about nowadays, as well as the better, more expensive ones. Some hang from a string around your neck, others have an adjustable or flexible stand, and there are even ones which clip directly onto your own spectacle frames.

My favourite is a small magnifier with a heavy base and adjustable spring clips to hold things with – as helpful as an extra hand. As ever, buy the best you can afford; you only have one pair of eyes, so look after them.

Many magnifiers, particularly the cheaper ones, have plastic lenses, and it is important these don't get scratched or you will soon be trying to see through a blur. It is useful to place the magnifier on a clean yellow duster to protect it from being scratched; this can also be used to keep it out of the sun.

MEASURING AND MARKING

For measuring accurately, use a good ruler. I find a metal one is best, as it will also serve as a straightedge for cutting along. You will need an HB pencil and an eraser, and, to ensure square corners, a set square of some kind. For marking out bricks and stones, a pointed tool of some kind is needed, such as an awl; but a fine-pointed defunct biro or even a cocktail stick can be used instead.

CRAFT KNIVES AND RAZOR SAWS

There are many types of craft knife available, from the cheap throwaway ones to those with surgical-quality scalpel-type blades. A razor saw and a small mitre block allow accurate cuts to be made fairly easily.

These items are often available as part of a 'craft set', which comes in a box to keep everything together. They usually contain a number of different-sized handles, a wide selection of blades, razor saw, mitre block, and sometimes an awl, tweezers, and sanders. They are produced by many manufacturers, varying in both quality and price. I like the ones made by X-acto, or the cheaper one by Draper. As with all equipment purchases, buy the best you can afford; it will provide the basic tools for a wide range of craft work for many years.

A typical craft set with interchangeable scalpel blades and handles. You will also need tweezers, if they are not included in your set.

TWEEZERS

Some craft sets include a pair of tweezers. If not, then these will be an essential addition to enable you to handle tiny bits easily, particularly for flower making. I couldn't manage without them, and have various sizes with different-shaped ends for different jobs.

MODELLING TOOLS

For dealing with the various modelling materials, such as Fimo and air-drying clay, I use whatever is handy and seems to suit the purpose: cocktail sticks, kebab skewers, paintbrush handles, manicure tools, even spoon handles. A leftover from when my children were young is a set of wooden tools originally used with Plasticine. Similar ones, intended for use with Fimo, can be bought from many model shops where Fimo is sold.

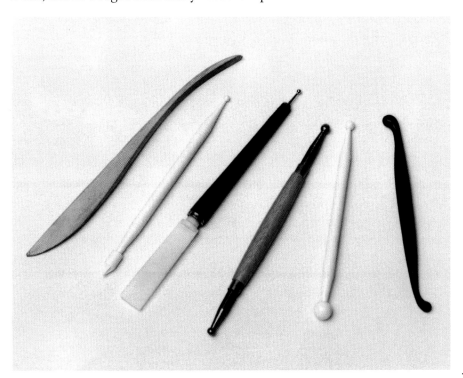

All sorts of tools, specially made or improvised, can be used for shaping modelling materials and forming paper flowers.

SUGARCRAFT TOOLS

Sugarcraft equipment suppliers sell a number of tools which are useful for modelling and flower making. Some of them are quite expensive, but I recently bought a reasonably priced plastic leaf veiner which has proved very useful, as the opposite end from what is intended as the 'business end' is nicely rounded, giving me two tools in one, for shaping the paper for flowers and leaves. There is a 'ball tool', with two different-sized ball ends, which is also useful for this, but if your paintbrush handles have rounded ends you can get away with using those.

FILES

Other tools which are helpful, but not essential, for shaping wood and other model materials, are small files. Some of mine were bought in a plastic wallet, which is handy, as they can be hung on the wall out of harm's way but are still easily accessible. These were sold as 'warding files', and each one has its own wooden handle. There are smaller, finer files, called 'needle files', but these are usually quite expensive.

PLIERS

A small pair of long-nose pliers is very useful for bending stiff wire, thin metal strip, and pins. They are also useful for holding wire or pushing it into places that your hands are too big to get into.

If you resort to using scissors for cutting wire, then make sure that it is an old pair, and that you keep them separate and only use them for this purpose. Tie a piece of coloured thread or tape around one handle so that you can recognize them easily.

SCISSORS AND WIRE CUTTERS

You will need very sharp scissors to cut paper and silk for flowers. I find that a good-quality pair with small, thin blades is best. It is surprising how difficult it is to cut paper cleanly if the scissors are not sharp.

Cutting wire easily needs wire cutters or side-cutters. You can use scissors, but this will spoil the cutting edge, which will quickly become uneven and jagged, so that cutting paper successfully becomes impossible.

PUNCHES

For many flowers I use circles of paper of various sizes, which are either cut out with scissors or punched out. I am fortunate in having a husband from whom I can borrow tools, amongst which are a number of different-sized hollow punches. This saves me a lot of time when I'm making a large number of flowers, but the cost of these would probably be prohibitive, unless you intend making wholesale quantities of flowers!

One punch which I find invaluable for producing large numbers of tiny circles of paper for making flowers is the office-style punch used to make holes in paper for filing. The holes are about ¼in (6.4mm) in diameter and the bits punched out, which are usually thrown away, are ideal for many flowers. These punches can be bought very cheaply from most stationers.

I use many different things to hold bits together until the glue sets: elastic bands of various sizes and widths, bulldog clips, crocodile clips, and spring clothes pegs, to name but a few.

CLAMPS

Miniature clamps and sash cramps are very useful to hold joints firmly in place until the glue sets and, though not essential, they can save a lot of time – not to mention the frayed temper, when things don't stick together properly. Model shops may have these, or they can be bought by mail order from such firms as Hobby's. These are, however, somewhat of a 'luxury' item: nice if you have them, but hardly worth the expense if you are only interested in making miniature gardens.

ABRASIVES

There is a very wide range of different abrasive papers available, from very coarse sandpaper to extremely fine flour paper, and some kind of abrasive is essential to smooth rough edges and get a good finish. There are times, however, when the most practical answer to getting at an awkward bit is to use emery boards from the cosmetics department.

If you have any old, worn emery boards, scrape the surface as smooth as possible and glue a piece of wet-and-dry paper on. When the glue is dry, trim to shape with scissors, and you have a purpose-made abrasive board.

DRILLS

For some items you will need to make holes, and to do this successfully may mean borrowing a small hand drill and drill bits, if you don't have one. A useful alternative is a hand-operated tool called a 'pin chuck', which is a sort of small hand-held drill chuck and handle. This, and a few small drill bits which can be fitted into the chuck, are all that is necessary for making the holes you will need. They can usually be bought at model shops or by mail order. You may, however, be able to improvise by using an awl or a very large darning needle.

STYROFOAM TRAYS

To shape many of the paper flowers I find it is necessary to work on a small piece of thin plastic foam, or spongy material of some kind. Some of the firm but slightly spongy plastic foam trays, like takeaway trays, which regularly turn up as supermarket food packaging, are very useful. If you can get a few new takeaway trays, perhaps from your local fish-and-chip shop or Chinese takeaway, these are ideal; but much of the supermarket packaging can be reused if carefully washed and allowed to dry.

NEEDLES AND PINS

A packet of different-sized darning needles is another invaluable item, for making holes in paper, and arranging flower petals. Straight pins from the haberdashery counter or stationers' are ideal for applying very tiny dabs of glue exactly where it is wanted. Those with a larger plastic head, which makes them easier to hold, are particularly useful. They can also be used to hold things in place temporarily when assembling models, and can even be used as parts of flowers!

COCKTAIL STICKS

Wooden cocktail sticks serve a number of useful purposes, such as stirring paint, applying small dabs of glue, putting a blob of thickish paint in the centre of a flower, and marking bricks or stones on styrofoam blocks, as mentioned earlier.

ESSENTIALS

Don't get the idea that you need to spend a small fortune on tools and equipment to enjoy making miniature garden projects. I use equipment because I have it already, not because it is absolutely essential to the task, although it does often make it easier and save time.

The craft set mentioned above, a metal ruler, set square, pencil, tweezers, scissors, and a sheet of abrasive paper are the only things really necessary for most jobs. Apart from the baseboards (which can usually be bought cut to size), the projects can be accomplished using just these tools – so you see, it doesn't have to be that expensive.

CHAPTER 5

METHODS

BASEBOARDS

All the projects are made using a baseboard of 9mm (³/₈in) thick MDF (medium density fibreboard). This can be bought from the local DIY shop, and they will often cut it to size for you, although there may be a small extra charge for cutting. If you cut it yourself, be very careful, as the dust from this board is very fine and can be a hazard to lungs, so wearing a mask of some kind is advisable.

Alternative materials could be plywood, chipboard, or other composition board, which, again, can often be had cut to size.

NEATENING EDGES

After you have finished your garden layout, it is a good idea to neaten the edges of the baseboard by adding a wooden edging. I suggest that you use obeche, or similar wood strip, about ¹/₈in (3.2mm) thick and ¹/₂in (12.7mm) wide. For the sides you will need two pieces the same length as the side of the baseboard, and for the front and back edges you will need two pieces the length of the front plus ¹/₄in (6.4mm) (or twice the thickness of the wood strip you are using), so that they will cover the ends of the side pieces neatly.

Alternatively, for a really professional look, you can make mitred joints at the corners. To do this you will need to cut the strips longer, to allow for the mitring. Cut the ends of the wood strip at an angle of 45° in opposite directions for each corner, so that they form a 90° angle when fixed together. If you have a mitre block, as shown on page 24, this will make the job much easier. Make sure that the shorter side of the wood strip is the same size as the baseboard edge, or it won't fit. Half-round beading with mitred corners also makes a very neat edging, as seen in the Trellis Arch project (page 60).

Colour the wood strip with stain, or paint it the colour of your choice, and glue the strips carefully round the edges, making sure that the corners are as neat as possible. When the glue has dried, finish with a coat of clear acrylic varnish.

Some projects, such as the Cottage Garden in Chapter 13 (page 112), use large grass areas; on these the grass mat material can be carried over the edges of the baseboard and stuck firmly underneath. This also provides protection for any surface on which the model may be stood.

If the garden is to be displayed on a polished surface, small pieces of craft felt glued to the underside of the baseboard will protect that surface from scratching. A piece of craft felt, the same size as the baseboard, glued to the whole of the underneath, is better, and can cover a multitude of errors as well.

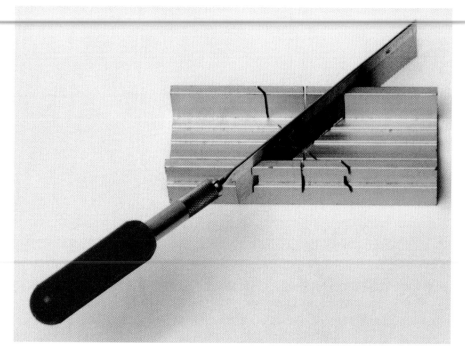

A razor saw and appropriately sized mitre block will greatly assist in cutting accurate joints in wood.

PLANS

It is not possible to print the baseboard plans full size in this book, so if you want to follow the projects exactly you will have to enlarge the plans.

ENLARGING PLANS

The plans are shown against a squared background so that you can enlarge the drawings fairly easily. Each square on the printed plan represents a 1in (25mm) square on the finished model, so your squares will have to be 1in squares, for the enlarged plans to end up the right size. Graph paper can be useful for this, if you buy large sheets marked in inches. Large stationers' often have this, usually in rolls of three sheets of paper. Otherwise, you will have to make your own enlargement paper.

Alternatively, plans can be enlarged on a photocopier if you have access to a suitable machine (but do remember that designs in this book are copyright and may not be reproduced commercially without the author's consent).

MAKING ENLARGEMENT PAPER

You can make your own squared enlargement paper, using a sheet of strong tracing paper larger than the overall size given for the plan you want to enlarge.

Rule a straight line right across the top, and then successive lines exactly 1in (25mm) below each other and parallel to the first line. Using a set square to ensure that the first line is at right angles, draw vertical lines from the top to the bottom of the paper, all exactly 1in (25mm) away from each other all the way across the paper, so that you have a piece of paper covered in squares of exactly 1 x 1in (25 x 25mm).

If you are likely to want to use more than one of the printed plans, then you can save yourself having to make a separate sheet of squared enlargement paper for each, by making one piece of squared paper which is bigger than any of the full-size plans. Stick this to a piece of card, to strengthen it, so that it can be used over and over again.

Use strong tracing paper to make your enlargements, and pin this over the squared paper so that you can see the squares through the tracing paper. Using these as a guide, draw first the outside edges of the plan, then the remaining lines of the design, as detailed below. Remove the pins, and you have your enlargement; and the squared paper can be reused.

MAKING THE ENLARGEMENT

You can now enlarge the plan by copying the relative position of each line on the printed plan to the same relative position on the squares of your enlargement plan. For instance, if a flowerbed outline crosses about a third of the way along the bottom of the 2nd square along and the 4th square down on the plan, it should cross about a third of the way along the bottom of the 2nd square along and the 4th square down on your enlargement also. Similarly, a line on the printed drawing which crosses around the middle of the left-hand side of the 2nd square along and the 4th square down will need to cross about the middle of the left-hand side of the 2nd square along and the 4th square down on your enlargement.

This looks complicated when put into words, but is actually quite simple. Work methodically through the squares on the printed drawing and mark onto your enlargement the relative positions where each line crosses a square. Join these together with as smooth a line as possible to give a larger version of the shape shown on the printed drawing.

TRANSFERRING PLANS

To transfer the plan to the baseboard, and to any 'grass' or other material required, you can use carbon paper, but this cannot be erased satisfactorily from material. I find dressmakers' tracing paper from the sewing shop easier to remove, but it is better to mark the 'wrong side' or underneath of grass material so that lines don't have to be removed at all.

Provided that you have made your enlargement on strong tracing paper, you can lay the enlargement the right way up on the baseboard, with your carbon paper between the tracing paper and the baseboard, and go over the lines of your plan with a pencil to transfer it to the baseboard. Then, for an area of grass material, the enlargement can be placed the *wrong* way up over the *wrong* side of your grass material, with the carbon paper between, and the relevant part similarly transferred. This way the lines won't show on the right side.

Enlarging plans by the grid method

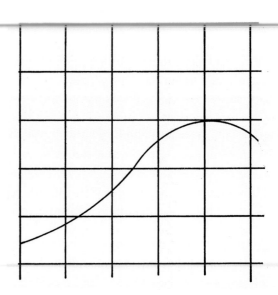

1 Position of line as shown on printed plan

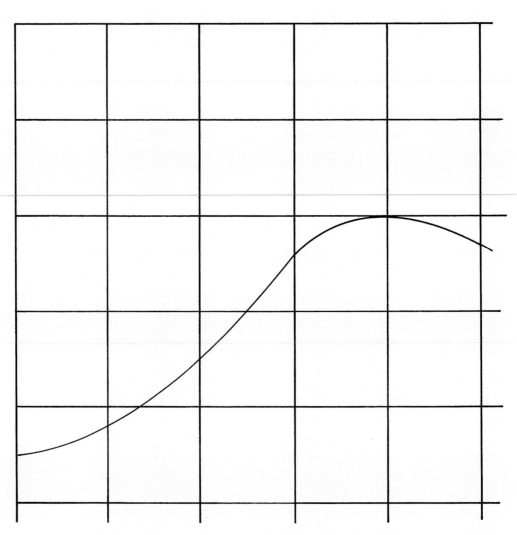

2 Relative position of the same line when enlarged to full size

SQUARING JIG

A 'jig' is the name given to any device used to help in positioning things for cutting or assembly. You will find it helpful for some of the projects if you make a small jig to help keep parts square during the assembly of such things as the trellis arch, bench seat, and so on.

All you need is a flat piece of 9mm ($^3/_8$in) thick MDF, or similar, about 10in (254mm) square, and two pieces of $^1/_4$in (6.4mm) square wood about 8in (203mm) long.

Use a set square to draw an accurate right angle about $^1/_2$in (12.7mm) away from two adjacent edges of one corner of the board. Then apply wood glue to one side of each of the lengths of square wood and fix them firmly in place along these lines. Check that they are absolutely square, and leave them for the glue to set hard. If you wish, you can also use small panel pins to hold the wood strips in place, but check that they are still square after pinning.

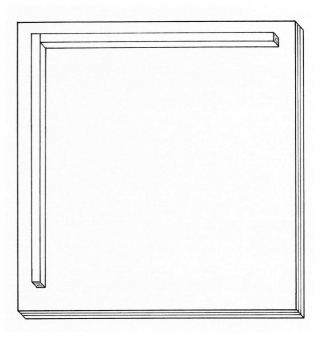

A home-made squaring jig.

MINIATURE SPRAY BOOTH

As we saw in Chapter 2 (page 11), using sprays is an ideal way to paint large numbers of very small items such as flowers. To prevent the 'overspray' from damaging the surrounding area, a cardboard box makes a very good miniature spray booth. Things to be sprayed can then either be stood inside the box, or better still suspended from the centre of the top of the box so as to hang inside without touching anything.

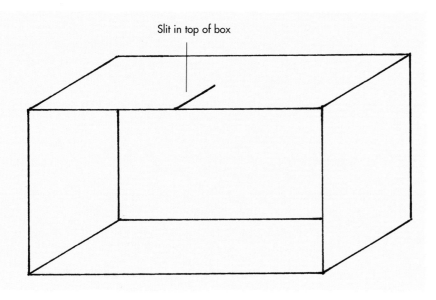

Slit in top of box

A spray booth improvised from a cardboard box.

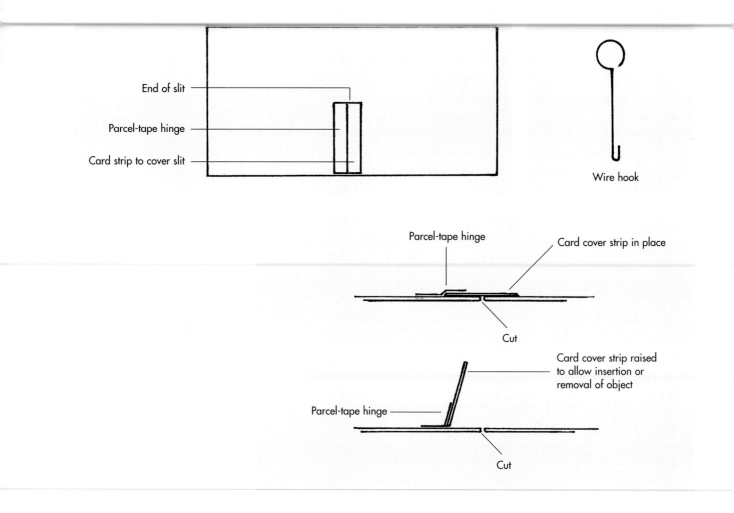

End of slit

Parcel-tape hinge

Card strip to cover slit

Wire hook

Parcel-tape hinge

Card cover strip in place

Cut

Card cover strip raised to allow insertion or removal of object

Parcel-tape hinge

Cut

To make a spray booth, lay a fairly large cardboard box on its side and cut a slit in what is now the top of the box, from the middle of the front to halfway across towards the back. Then cut a spare piece of card about 2in (51mm) wide and just long enough to cover the slit. This is stuck on top of the box, along one side of the slit, with parcel tape, leaving just a tiny bit of the slit at the centre of the box uncovered, and means that the slot can be covered up when spraying, but the card can be lifted and turned back to facilitate the removal of items which have been hung inside for spraying.

This is, obviously, a very cheap, quick way of making a spray booth, and when the box gets too covered in paint, you can just throw it away and make another one.

So that I can turn things to spray all round them, I use a piece of wire to hang them on. This is bent at one end to hold whatever I am spraying, and the other end is bent into a loop, which forms a handle to hold on to above the top of the slit, and also stops it from falling straight through. This lets me turn the item round and about to cover it with spray, without getting painted fingers in the process. The wire holding the item can then be moved out through the slot, complete with the sprayed article, and hung up for drying, without you having to touch any part which may have paint on it.

CHAPTER 6

SIMPLE PLANTS

Many plants can be made quite simply, by gluing together various bits and pieces such as reindeer moss, stamens, dried plant material, and silk flowers. You don't have to make anything from scratch, just cut and stick.

ROCKERY PLANTS

You can buy reindeer moss in a wide variety of colours now (see page 15). This can be used on its own for many plants, including clumps of rockery plants or trailing plants such as aubretia and alyssum; or the green variety may be used as a basis for plant clumps, to which various things can be added for the flowers.

All these plants and more can be made using the simple techniques described in this chapter.

Reindeer moss and flock is one of the simplest ways of making rockery or ground-cover plants.

The flowers in this reindeer-moss plant are made from artificial stamens.

One way of creating a low-growing, flowering clump is to use green reindeer moss, put dabs of tacky glue on what is to be the top of the clump, and press it lightly into a small heap of suitably coloured railway layout scenic material, then set it aside to dry.

Another type of clump of small flowers can be made using tiny artificial stamens (see page 15). They usually come with a stamen head on each end of a short stem piece. Cut the stems down to leave about ¹/₂in (12.7mm) beyond the stamen head, and stick them into the clumps of reindeer moss with tacky glue. I find it easiest to have a small pool of tacky glue in a foil tray and use tweezers to pick up the tiny stamens, dip the stem end into the tacky glue, and then stick it into the piece of reindeer moss.

Individual flowers of sea lavender, coloured as you choose, or bits of dried statice, can also be stuck to reindeer moss with tacky glue to make effective clumps of low-growing flowers.

Sea lavender and other dried flowers can also be combined with reindeer moss to make convincing low-level plants.

For taller plants, use aquarium greenery with dried flower materials . . .

. . . or with small silk flowers.

POT PLANTS

Many different plants can be made by using little bits of dried grasses or tiny dried flowers – either just as they are or coloured with fabric paint, poster paint, acrylic paint, or food colouring. These can be glued to green reindeer moss, or bunched together with aquarium greenery, and the ends bound together firmly with florists' stem tape, then planted in pots. An alternative is to use small silk flowers and aquarium greenery.

LARGER PLANTS AND BUSHES

Some synthetic aquarium plants are suitable for use as bushes more or less as they are. The colour can be varied a little by the judicious use of a very fine dusting with matt spray paint. This must be just a very quick pass over the leaves, or they will be too heavily covered. Variegated-leaf plants can be created by painting the centres or edges of the plastic leaves.

Paint the edges or centres of aquarium greenery leaves to give the effect of variegated foliage.

A small bush made with flock material and wire.

Satisfactory plants and bushes can also be made from railway layout foam flock material, which is available in various sizes and colours (see page 16). To do this, cut pieces of covered wire a suitable length for the size of bush you want to make. A small plastic bag is best for holding the flock material you intend to use, or you could use a fairly deep glass dish. Using one length of wire at a time, coat this with tacky glue for about two-thirds of its length. Insert the glued end of wire into the flock material and roll it about to pick up bits of flock on the glue. Remove the wire from the flock, and push the uncoated end into a block of Oasis or Dryfoam, to hold it safely until the glue dries. Repeat this with the other lengths of wire. When the glue has dried, give the wires a gentle shake to remove any bits which haven't stuck properly.

If you think that the wire hasn't picked up enough flock, you can add further dabs of glue and repeat until it is sufficiently well covered. Bunch a number of the 'flocked' wires together, and twist the uncoated ends of wire together firmly for the main stem. The flocked wires can then be bent and arranged to form a bush, trailing plant, or climber. If you wish, the twisted stem part can be covered with florists' stem tape to give a smoother appearance.

For flowering bushes, add coloured foam flock material. After covering wires with green flock as above, add sparse dabs of tacky glue and dip the ends of wire which have already been covered with flock into the coloured flock material to pick up a little for the flowers.

A suitable piece of bare hedgerow twig can be turned into a bush or small tree by attaching flock material in a similar way as for the wires, but you will need a larger plastic bag to hold the flock as the whole thing has to be dipped in.

Twigs can also be turned into bushes by gluing pieces of green reindeer moss to them with tacky glue. For flowering bushes, add coloured flock material to the reindeer moss bush. Apply dabs of glue to the surface of the moss and dip it into a bag of coloured flock material. Another alternative is to glue bits of dried flower material to the reindeer moss bush.

Reindeer moss and natural twigs make a different kind of bush

This attractive plant combines aquarium-greenery leaves with variegated paper flowers made as described in the next chapter

CHAPTER 7

BASIC FLOWER-MAKING TECHNIQUES

Many of the materials and tools included here have already been mentioned in earlier chapters, but as the aim of this chapter is to explain the basic techniques for making many of the flowers shown in the following projects, some duplication is unavoidable and, I hope, forgivable.

PAPER FLOWERS

Many of the flowers in my miniature gardens are made from circles of paper, mostly using either of two basic methods: what I call the 'paper circle and stamen' method, and the 'floret' method. In this chapter I will explain what these two methods are, and in the next chapter tell you how these basic methods can be used to create specific types of flowers.

Making flowers can be messy, so work on a large sheet of paper or an old cloth, to make gathering up all the bits a lot easier. A large tray with a raised edge helps to keep all the bits together. It also stops tools rolling onto the floor, and saves a lot of time and frustration as you search for small bits on hands and knees! If you are working where the floor is carpeted, it also helps avoid the danger of bits of wire, pins, or needles falling onto the floor and sticking into the carpet fibres.

Many types of flower can be made from paper by the methods described in this chapter.

PAPER CIRCLE AND STAMEN

For this example, cut circles of coloured craft tissue paper about ³/₈in (9.5mm) in diameter, and select small, round-headed artificial stamens.

DISHED CIRCLES

Many flowers have a centre which is 'dished' – that is, curved inwards – to a greater or lesser degree. To dish your paper circle, use a suitable round-ended tool, either a modelling or sugarcraft tool (see page 20), or an improvised tool such as an artist's paintbrush handle with a rounded end. Work on a piece of thin synthetic foam material, and press the centre of the circle onto it with the tool, then work the tool gently in tiny circular movements until the paper is sufficiently dished. If you are too energetic with this the paper will tear, but you will soon get the feel of when enough is enough!

To keep the flower safe until the glue dries, push the stem into a block of Oasis. If the stamen has a soft stem, you may first have to make a hole in the Oasis with a darning needle, and then push the stem into this.

ASSEMBLING A SINGLE FLOWER

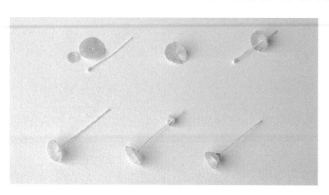

To assemble a single flower, use a darning needle, or something similar, to make a hole in the centre of a dished paper circle, and from the concave side (the pushed-in side) thread the stem end of the stamen through the hole. I find tweezers invaluable for handling all these little bits, but if you are very nimble-fingered you may be able to manage without. Apply a tiny blob of tacky glue to the centre of the paper circle, so that the base of the stamen head sticks to it. A large-headed pin or a cocktail stick is useful for this.

Stages in making a single flower by the circle and stamen method.
1 The materials: stamen, coloured circle, small green paper circle.
2 Flower circle dished.
3 Dished circle threaded onto stamen.
4 Dished circle stuck to stamen head.
5 Small green circle added.
6 The completed single flower

Most flowers have green sepals behind their petals, so I usually add a green circle, smaller than the flower circles used, to the back of the flower circle, and stick it to both the flower and the stamen stem with just the tiniest touch of glue; I then paint the stamen green to blend in with the sepals.

ASSEMBLING A DOUBLE FLOWER

For what are generally called 'double' or 'semi-double' flowers, you will need more than one layer of paper. Start with one circle of paper, as for a single flower. Then add another paper circle to the back of this and stick the centre of it to the previous layer with a tiny touch of tacky glue next to the stem. Add more layers in a similar way, until the flower reaches the degree of fullness you want, and finish with a small green circle for the sepals, as for the single flower. Various kinds of flowers can be made in this way, depending on the size and number of the paper circles used.

Stages in making a double flower by the same method.
1 Stamen, coloured circles, small green circle.
2 Coloured circles threaded onto stamen.
3 The completed double flower.

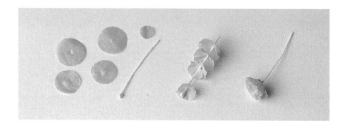

BUDS

For partly open buds, use circles of tissue paper and a slightly larger stamen than used for the flowers above. Start as if making a single flower, but this time apply tacky glue to the stamen head, squeeze the paper circle gently to press it onto the stamen, and cover the whole of the stamen head. Thread another paper circle onto the stamen stem and apply glue to the lower half of the stamen head. Taking hold of the stamen stem just below the paper, roll gently between finger and thumb to stick the paper to the lower half of the already covered stamen head and give a bud shape, but leave the outer edge of the paper circle free. Add a small green circle behind this for the sepals. Apply tacky glue, and roll gently between finger and thumb, as above, to cover part of the stem and the bottom half of the bud. Set aside for the glue to dry, then gently ease out the free edge of the coloured paper circle at the top of the bud with a darning needle or similar implement. If you make a number of buds in this way, ease out more or less of the edges on each bud to give varying degrees of opening.

Closed buds can be made by using just a green circle and a stamen, in the same way as the first stage above, so that the green circle covers the whole of the stamen head. The finished shape of buds will vary depending on the shape of the stamen used.

FLORET METHOD

I use this method for plants which need a number of very small flowers for each flower head, or for those which need trumpet-shaped flowers, either singly or grouped together.

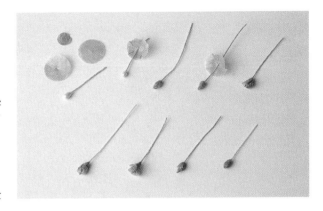

Stages in making buds by the circle and stamen method.
1 Stamen, coloured circles, small green circle.
2 Dished coloured circle threaded onto stamen.
3 Stamen covered with coloured circle.
4 Second coloured circle threaded onto stamen.
5 Second circle partially stuck to already covered stamen.
6 Small green circle added to back of bud.
7 Edges of coloured circle teased out to form part-open bud.
8 A tight bud using only one coloured circle to cover the stamen, and one small green circle.
9 A closed bud using only a small green circle to cover the stamen.

Making flowers by the floret method. A blunt-pointed skewer is being used to press the paper circle into the styrofoam tray. In the foreground: paper circles at left, florets at right.

MAKING FLORETS

MAKING FLORETS

Many of the flowers made by this method use what I think of as a 'small circle'. By this I mean about ¼in (6.4mm) in diameter, which is where using an office-style punch can be a great time-saver. To form the florets, each circle of paper is pushed into the plastic foam of something like a takeaway tray.

Place the tip of a fairly blunt-pointed instrument, such as a wooden kebab skewer, in the centre of the circle, press and twist at the same time. This should push the paper partially into the foam, which will shape it and hold it in place as well. The tool used should not have too sharp a point, or the paper will be torn. Florets can be formed quite quickly this way, after a little practice.

If you want them for a flower requiring tight florets, leave them in the foam until you are ready for assembly; otherwise, use tweezers to remove them gently, and store them in small containers, a separate one for each colour, until you are ready to assemble your flowers.

Be warned: for many flowers you will need lots of florets. It is a good idea to spend an hour or so making lots of florets of different colours, including some greens, so that you have a ready-made supply to hand when it comes to assembling your flowers or plants.

FADING

The colours of tissue paper, napkins, and crepe paper all fade in bright sunlight, so avoid displaying gardens where this could be a problem. The colours of paper are also easily damaged by dampness. I have found that spraying paper flowers with Krylon Crystal Clear makes them less fragile, and enables dust to be blown off more easily. It also seems to retard the fading of colours slightly, and as it is also water-resistant it protects them from damage by dampness.

THREAD FLOWERS

I use various kinds of thread, depending on the type of flower: crochet cotton, of various thicknesses, and stranded embroidery threads are the most useful.

GENERAL METHOD FOR THREAD FLOWERS

Cut a length of covered wire about 4in (102mm) long for the stem. Hold this alongside a paintbrush handle, or something similar, preferably slightly tapered and approximately ⁵⁄₁₆in (7.9mm) in diameter for a largish flower, or thinner for a smaller flower.

Select a colour of crochet cotton which is suitable for the type of flower. Hold the end of the cotton firmly against the wire, and wind the thread around both the wire and the paintbrush handle a number of times. The number of turns needed will vary, depending on the type of flower wanted. Experiment with different numbers of turns, starting with about 25 for crochet cotton, or about half this number for embroidery thread. Cut off the end of the thread, leaving about 1in (25mm). A couple of turns of green embroidery thread can be added on top of the other thread, to provide the

A few turns of thread will give a simple, daisy-like flower; use a larger amount of thread for a densely petalled flower like chrysanthemum.

green sepals to the back of the flower, and these should be trimmed shorter than the coloured petals when finishing off the flower.

Bend back the wire on either side of the thread and twist firmly together. The easiest way is to hold the wires together, close to the thread, and turn the brush round to twist the wires.

Remove the brush handle or other implement used and, holding the loops of thread tightly together, wind the shorter of the two ends of wire round the thread next to the stem to form the base of the flower. Cut the loops and trim the cut ends, as necessary, to give a good shape. A small dab of tacky glue in the centre, over the wire loop, helps to stop bits coming out.

To fix the thread petals in place, spray with fixative, then arrange the thread to form a suitable flower shape, giving additional short bursts of spray as necessary. To curl the thread petals, spray them as above, and roll them around a kebab stick or cocktail stick whilst still damp; again, spray and respray as necessary.

Don't forget the safety rules (see page 11) for working with sprays.

Stages in making a thread flower.

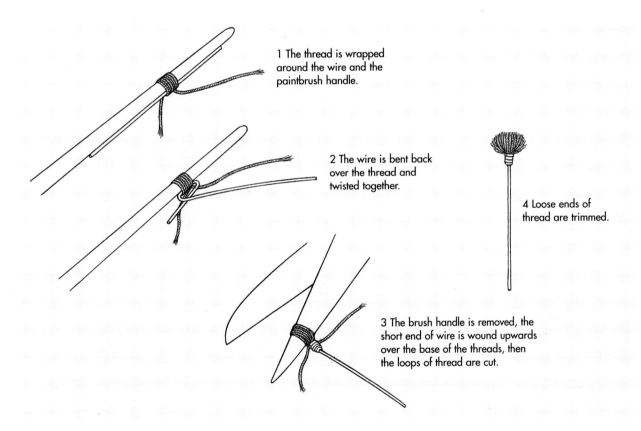

1 The thread is wrapped around the wire and the paintbrush handle.

2 The wire is bent back over the thread and twisted together.

3 The brush handle is removed, the short end of wire is wound upwards over the base of the threads, then the loops of thread are cut.

4 Loose ends of thread are trimmed.

LEAVES AND GREENERY

Much of the wide variety of synthetic greenery sold by pet shops and stores for use in aquariums is very suitable for leaves of flowers and plants (see page 16), and can be used more or less as it is, or cut up and stuck together in different arrangements using a suitable glue. Making leaf shapes yourself is another option.

MAKING LEAVES

If you want to make leaves yourself, then one way is to use large fabric leaves, either bought new or recycled from ones you already have. Another method is to cut up printed fabric with leaves on it. Although the leaves are inevitably too large to use as they are, at least the colour is usually about right, and one leaf can be cut up into many smaller ones.

With either method the same approach is used. Before cutting any fabric you must coat the back of it with some form of 'fray stop' and allow it to dry completely, so that when you cut the material you don't end up with a shaggy mess because the fabric has frayed. There are proprietary fray-stop products available, but you can also use PVA glue diluted about half-and-half with water. Although some bought silk leaves are made from fabric which has already been treated to prevent fraying, I find it is still advisable to treat them, just in case. Once the fabric has dried completely, you can cut out leaves of whatever shape and size you want, and some suggested patterns are given in Chapter 8.

If the fabric is a bit floppy and you feel it needs to be stiffened, or if you want it to set in a particular shape, use a proprietary fabric stiffener, following the manufacturer's instructions. I use one called Stiffy, which I simply paint on, but you could also use spray starch.

Leaves can also be made from paper, and indeed, for many kinds, this is both the easiest way and the most effective. You can use the 'floret' method (see page 36), with green paper circles, for the leaves of plants like ivy-leafed geraniums, for example (see page 177). For others – nasturtiums, for instance – a paper circle, sometimes dished, serves quite well. Crepe paper is useful where you want to curl the leaf, as the stretch in the paper makes this quite a simple job. For a poppy leaf, for example, cut the appropriate shape from crepe paper, lay it on a piece of thin foam, and draw down the centre of the leaf, lengthways, with a cocktail stick. The amount of pressure you put onto it will determine the degree of curl. One of the disadvantages of crepe paper is that the colours are easily damaged by dampness or bright sunlight, but Krylon Crystal Clear acrylic spray can be used to advantage (see page 36).

Fimo can also be used for making leaves. You will need to mix colours together to give a suitable shade of green, and it can then be either pressed, rolled, or pinched to become as thin as possible. The shapes given in the patterns can be used with Fimo as well as with fabric or paper, the leaves being placed carefully in a baking tin lined with foil or baking parchment (see tip on page 11), or on ovenproof glassware. After baking, the Fimo leaves are used in the same way as the others.

For some purposes you will need to stick a fine piece of covered wire down the centre of each leaf, whether they are made of paper, fabric, or even Fimo, either so that they can be grouped together, or to make them easier to attach to the plant; but for some types of plants, the leaves are stuck directly onto the flower stems.

As you will realize, making leaves by hand is time-consuming and fiddly, particularly where small leaves are required in large numbers, so for many of these I often take the easy option and use aquarium greenery.

CHAPTER 8

MAKING
SPECIFIC FLOWERS

Creating a general impression of a group of flowers or an anonymous plant is relatively simple, but when you want to simulate a specific type of flower or plant it gets more complicated. This chapter explains how the general methods outlined in the previous chapter can be used to create particular types of flowers. 'Covered wire' means the kind used for sugarcraft work, unless specifically stated otherwise. The 'spray' referred to in this chapter can be hairspray, matt varnish spray, or Crystal Clear acrylic spray. If you wish to make your own leaves, patterns are given in this chapter. The general methods and basic techniques used are as detailed in the previous chapter. Use a tacky glue throughout.

An array of handmade flowers, all of them variations on the simple techniques described in the previous chapter.

PAPER FLOWERS

CIRCLE AND STAMEN METHOD

DOUBLE BEGONIA

MATERIALS

❀ Coloured tissue-paper circles varying in size from about $^7/_{16}$in (11.1mm) to $^5/_{16}$in (7.9mm) diameter
❀ Green tissue circles about $^3/_{16}$in (4.8mm) diameter
❀ Small round stamens
❀ Aquarium plant leaves, or handmade leaves

FLOWERS

Form the flowers as detailed on pages 33–4, using a number of layers of paper; a couple of circles of each of three different sizes is effective. Starting with the smallest circle nearest to the stamen head, add layers of increasing size before finishing with a small green circle at the back of the flower. When dry, arrange the edges of the circles with a darning needle to shape the flower and hide the stamen in the centre. Spray to fix.

BUDS

Make partly opened buds as detailed on page 35, using coloured circles about $^3/_8$in (9.5mm) diameter and green circles about $^1/_4$in (6.4mm) diameter. Spray to fix.

Camellia (top) and double begonias. A red camellia is shown on page 97.

ASSEMBLY

Form a short-stemmed plant by chopping up plastic aquarium plant with oval leaves about $^3/_8$in (9.5mm) long, and bunching them together with a number of flower and bud stems. Bind the bottom of the stems tightly with florists' stem tape to hold them firmly in place. Alternatively, use handmade leaves with a covered wire glued down the centre of each leaf, and bunch these together with flower and bud stems to form the plant.

Begonia leaf pattern.

CAMELLIA

MATERIALS

- ❀ Coloured tissue-paper circles varying in size from about ³/₈in (9.5mm) to ¼in (6.4mm) diameter
- ❀ Green tissue circles about ³/₁₆in (4.8mm) diameter
- ❀ Medium-sized round yellow stamens
- ❀ Aquarium mat greenery, or handmade leaves

FLOWERS

Form flowers and partly open buds as detailed on pages 33–5, but arrange the edges of the circles with a darning needle to shape the flower so that the stamen is *visible* on the fully open flowers. Spray to fix.

ASSEMBLY

Aquarium mat greenery with medium-sized darkish green oval leaves should be used for the bush. Trim the ends of the flower stems fairly short, then stick the flowers and buds to the greenery using a suitable clear glue designed for use with plastic. Handmade leaves could be used, stuck to a suitable piece of dried twig.

Camellia leaf pattern.

ROSES

There are many different kinds of roses, so they need to be assembled in different ways, all of which are variations of the circle and stamen method detailed on pages 33–5.

An effective colour variation can be made by using white, cream, yellow, or pink tissue paper for the circles, and colouring just the edges or centres with a felt-tip pen of a suitable contrasting colour. The fixing spray should slightly blur the dividing line between the two colours.

A hybrid tea rose with handmade paper leaves. By colouring your paper circles with a felt-tip pen you can make a rose with variegated petals.

Three roses: (left to right) hybrid tea, bush rose, and floribunda. A rambling rose can be seen by the house door on page 169.

HYBRID TEA ROSE

FLOWERS
For the centre of the flower, start with one of the smaller circles of coloured paper and work as if for a part-open bud (see page 35). Add another couple of circles a little larger, and stick them to the bottom half of the stamen. The larger circles can now be added, usually about three. Use small sharp scissors to make five or six snips around the last couple of circles, from the outside towards the centre of the flower. Finish with a green circle. When the glue is dry, arrange the edges of the circles with a darning needle and use a cocktail stick to curl the edges of the snips on the last circles towards the back of the flower. Spray to fix them.

BUDS
Make part-open buds in the normal way (see page 35), using coloured circles of about $^3/_8$in (9.5mm) diameter and the same stamens as for the flowers, finishing with a green circle of about $^1/_4$in (6.4mm) diameter.

ASSEMBLY
The simplest way is to use aquarium plant mat with small leaves for bushes, or make lots of handmade leaves, glued to covered wires in groups of five, and twist the wires together to form a bush. Cut the stamen stems short, about $^3/_{16}$in (4.8mm), and stick flowers and buds to the greenery with the appropriate glue.

Rose leaf pattern.

BUSH ROSE

Make the flowers and buds as for Camellia, above (see page 41), but assemble the bush as for the tea rose.

FLORIBUNDA ROSE

Make flowers and buds as given for either the bush rose above, or the hybrid tea rose, but use slightly smaller circles of paper.

ASSEMBLY

Use the same type of aquarium greenery as for the previous roses. Bunch a number of flower stems together, and apply tacky glue to the stems from about ¼in (6.4mm) below the flower heads to stick the stems together. When completely dry, cut the bunch of stems down to about ½in (12.7mm) long and glue to the bush with the appropriate glue.

RAMBLING ROSE

Make flowers and buds of any of the three types detailed above; but for the hybrid tea type of flowers, make the largest circles only ⅜in (9.5mm) diameter.

ASSEMBLY

The rose in Chapter 16 (see pages 174 and 176) uses tiny-leafed dried plant material, sprayed green. Alternatively, you could use plastic-coated garden wire for the main stems, stick individual handmade leaves onto fine, green-covered wires, then glue these to the main stems, which will need cutting to different lengths from 5in (127mm) to 8in (203mm). When completely dry, bunch the lower ends of the stems together and bind the lower 1in (25mm) tightly together with florists' tape. Now you can bring the rambler into bloom by gluing on the flowers and buds.

HOLLYHOCKS

Some hollyhocks have single flowers and some have semi-double or double flowers. One of mine has fine double pink flowers, others have deep red semi-double flowers, and some have single flowers of various colours. You decide which yours will be.

MATERIALS

- ❀ Coloured paper circles about ⅜in (9.5mm) diameter to ¼in (6.4mm)
- ❀ Green circles about ³⁄₁₆in (4.8mm) diameter for flowers and leaves (see text for alternatives), ⁵⁄₁₆in (7.9mm) for buds
- ❀ Medium-sized round stamens

FLOWERS

The flowers of some hollyhocks have petals with the centre a darker colour than the rest. These can be made by using felt pens to colour the centres of the flower circles before forming the flowers – pale creamy-yellow tissue with a dark plum-coloured centre is very striking. Make circle-and-stamen flowers as detailed on pages 33–5, either single or double, and of varying sizes.

A single stem of hollyhocks with semi-double flowers. Hollyhocks with single flowers can be seen in the Cottage Garden flowerbed on page 126.

Buds

Make some partly open buds, using coloured paper circles about $3/8$in (9.5mm) diameter, green paper circles about $5/16$in (7.9mm), and medium-sized round stamens. Some closed buds (see page 35) will also be needed, using medium-sized round stamens and green paper circles.

Assembly

Hollyhocks can be anything from 3ft (914mm) to 8ft (2438mm) tall, so you will need a stem of between 3in (76mm) and 8in (203mm) in length to be within scale size; and as these are tall flowers the stem needs to be fairly strong and sturdy, so use thick gauge covered wire. Cut the end of the stamen stems of one closed bud very short and stick it firmly to the top of the covered-wire stem for a terminal bud. Trim the ends of other buds, some closed, some partly open, and stick to the wire stem with tiny dabs of tacky glue below the terminal bud.

Start with closed buds and work down the stem with buds getting progressively more open as you go, and the stamen stems about $1/8$in (3.2mm) long. Stick them to left, right and centre of stem, until you have covered about a quarter of the way down. Now start introducing small flowers, working as above for the buds, but with stems about $1/4$in (6.4mm), and using flowers getting progressively larger, until about three quarters of the stem have been covered.

Push this completed flowering stem into a block of Oasis and leave until the glue has completely dried so that the flowers are not disturbed when adding the greenery. Spray to fix. Make more complete flower spikes in a similar way with stems of different lengths, some with all open flowers, so that no two stems are the same.

Leaves

Hollyhock leaf pattern.

When the flower spikes are completely dry you can add the greenery. Tiny bits of paper napkin are effective: cut circles about $3/16$in (4.8mm) diameter and make florets (see page 36). Stick these, with a trace of tacky glue, to the stem between the flowers; this will also serve to cover some of the stamen stems stuck to the flower stem. Alternatively, paint the back of a large silk leaf with fray-stop, and when dry cut tiny pieces to stick to the flower stem between the flowers. Basal leaves can be formed from a clump of suitably shaped aquarium greenery, and the flower spikes stuck into the flowerbed down through the centre. An alternative method is to make leaves from fabric or from Fimo to the shape given in the pattern. Bunch together a number of flower spikes and leaves, and bind florists' tape around the bottom of all the stems to keep them together.

ORNAMENTAL POPPY

MATERIALS

❀ Orange, red, pink, or mauve craft tissue circles, ¹/₂in (12.7mm) and ³/₈in (9.5mm) diameter
❀ Covered wire, 24 gauge
❀ Aquarium greenery
❀ Greyish-green spray paint
❀ Thick black acrylic paint
❀ Medium-sized oval stamens
❀ Paper napkins or crepe paper

FLOWERS

Cut two or three circles of tissue. About 4in (102mm) of covered wire will be needed for each stem. Form a small double loop at one end of the stem with pliers. Then make the flowers as described on pages 33–5, using the wire instead of a stamen, the loop serving as the stamen head. Add a blob of thick black paint to hide the wire and form the flower centre. When the paint is dry, spray to fix.

BUDS

For part-open buds, use medium-sized stamens and ¹/₂in (12.7mm) circles of paper. Make as detailed on page 35, finishing with a green circle, but stick the petals and the green circle to the sides of the stamen, squeezing together just above the top of the stamen. Closed buds can be made in the normal way, using a large oval stamen. Then bend the end of the stem over about ¹/₂in (12.7mm) from the bud end in a curve, so that the bud is pointing more or less downwards.

LEAVES

Poppy leaves need to be fixed at intervals up the flower and bud stems, and are greyish-green in colour. I use paper napkins or crepe paper, cutting different-sized leaves to an oval shape with a bit of a point at one end. Then glue a piece of fine covered wire down the centre, and use a cocktail stick to frill the edges of the leaves a bit. When the glue is completely dry, the ends of the covered wire are trimmed and the leaves stuck to the flower stems, small ones down to about halfway up and larger ones below. Leaves can also be made to the same sort of shape with Fimo, if you can get it thin enough without it falling apart.

Poppy leaf pattern.

ASSEMBLY

A bunch of flowers and buds can be bound together with florists' tape and large leaves stuck to the bottom bit to form a good-sized plant. An alternative way to form a plant is to select suitably shaped aquarium greenery to form a basal clump of leaves, and dust on a very fine mist of pale greyish-green paint. When the paint is dry, push the stems of some flowers and buds between the basal leaves. The ornamental poppy can be seen in the Cottage Garden on page 126.

One of the main distinctions between different kinds of flowers and plants is in the way they are assembled together: long stems or short, single flower heads or multiple flowers, for example, and the different types of leaves or plant shapes that go with them. For instance, the actual flower shape which will adequately represent a begonia, a camellia, and a bush rose is very much the same. Change the type of leaves, the length of the stems, and the general shape of the plant, and you can make a reasonable representation of any of these three.

FLORET METHOD

Zonal Pelargonium (Geranium)

MATERIALS

❀ Small plastic beads, preferably green, about ¹⁄₈in (3.2mm) diameter
❀ Green covered wire for flower stems
❀ Thicker wire for main plant stems
❀ Coloured paper circles, ¹⁄₄in (6.4mm) diameter, in pinks, reds, mauve, and white
❀ Green circles, ³⁄₁₆in (4.8mm) and ¹⁄₄in (6.4mm) diameter, for leaves – or aquarium greenery

A group of pelargoniums in a subtle range of colours. Compare the trailing geraniums in the window boxes on page 176.

FLOWERS

Cut flower stems about 1½in (38.1mm) long and stick a bead on one end of each one with tacky glue, pushing the end of the wire into the hole in the bead if possible. Push the ends of the stems into a block of Oasis to let the glue set firmly and to keep them safe while you make the flowers.

If you only want short, upright-stemmed plants, grouped together in a flowerbed, then an alternative is to use fairly long plastic-headed pins as a basis for the flower head. I recently bought a plastic box full from the supermarket and used these with red paper florets to good effect.

Make lots of florets (see page 36), using ¼in (6.4mm) circles of paper. This is where using an office-type punch saves time, as you will need 8 or more florets for each flower head, and a number of flower heads for each plant, so you could need 50 or 60 florets for a large plant!

The florets are stuck to the bead flower head (or plastic pin head) with tacky glue. Put a blob of tacky glue on a small foil dish or greaseproof paper bun case, pick up a floret with tweezers, holding it by the outside edge, dip the base into the glue, and then press it onto the bead. Arrange the florets to cover the bead evenly.

I find it easiest to use a small piece of Oasis to hold one flower stem at a time during assembly of the flower, and place the completed flower heads in another block until ready to assemble the plant.

LEAVES

One way to make suitable leaves is to cut aquarium greenery leaves to a roundish shape and form a low plant, then stick in the flower stalks, trimming to length as necessary. Alternatively, make the leaves from tissue-paper circles. These, I think, look more convincing. Use green tissue circles, a few only ³⁄₁₆in (4.8mm) diameter and a few ⁵⁄₁₆in (7.9mm), but mostly ¼in (6.4mm) punched ones.

Zonal pelargonium leaf pattern.

Many geraniums have distinct markings, or zones, on the leaves, which is why they are properly called *zonal pelargoniums*. To simulate this, use felt-tip pens to make roughly circular or horseshoe-shaped markings on the paper circles for the leaves, before you start on the plants. Take care, when assembling, that all the leaves on one plant are of the same kind and colour!

The leaves also look best when dished off-centre. To do this, use a medium-sized ball tool or a rounded paintbrush handle. Place it near the edge of the circle, then press and twist slightly to dish the leaf. Cut covered wire stems about 1in (25mm) to 1½in (38.1mm) long. Handling them with tweezers, stick the leaves to the stems with a tiny dab of tacky glue: a small leaf at the top, and larger ones below. If you hold the leaf by the edge furthest from the dishing, put the glue on the underside of the leaf at the opposite side, then press the glued bit against the stem, it should attach itself quite well; and although there are no individual leaf stems as such, it will look reasonably realistic.

ASSEMBLY

Bunch together a number of stems with flowers all the same colour, and a number of stems of leaves. Bind them with florists' tape, sewing cotton, or very fine wire to keep the bunch together. A bit of glue put on the stems first also helps. Holding the bunch firmly, and with the aid of tweezers, the stems can now be bent a bit and arranged into a reasonable geranium plant.

TRAILING GERANIUMS (IVY-LEAFED GERANIUMS)

FLOWERS

Trailing geraniums can be made using a modification of the method for making ordinary geraniums. Make lots of florets, as before, but instead of creating flower heads, stick them to the leaf stems during assembly.

LEAVES

These plants are often called 'ivy-leafed' geraniums, so for the leaves I use the 'floret' method, with green circles of $^3/_{16}$in (4.8mm), $^1/_4$in (6.4mm) and $^5/_{16}$in (7.9mm) diameter – make plenty of green florets.

Trailing (ivy-leafed) geranium leaf pattern.

ASSEMBLY

Covered wires varying in length from about 3in (76mm) to 2in (51mm) will be needed for the main stems, and 1in (25mm) lengths for side stems.

Take one long stem to start with, and two or three side stems. Bend the bottom $^1/_8$in (3.2mm) of the side stems at an angle, and glue these to the main stem at intervals. Now clothe the stems with leaves. Use the small green florets at the ends of stems and the larger ones further down, except for the bottom $^3/_4$in (19.1mm) of the main stem, which should be left free of leaves. Stick the green florets to the stems with a dab of tacky glue on the back of each floret.

To add the flowers, stick coloured paper florets to the stems between the leaves, in groups of five or six. An alternative would be to stick the floret groups to very short pieces of covered wire and then stick the covered-wire flower stems to the leaf stems, but the extra effort is not necessary to give an effective result.

Two or three completed pieces should be enough to bunch together to form a large display of cascading geraniums; bind the leafless ends together tightly with florists' stem tape. If this end is planted firmly, you can use tweezers to bend the foliage-covered stems into position so as to spill over the sides of planters, troughs, etc.

DELPHINIUM

MATERIALS

* ❀ Craft tissue or paper napkin circles about $^1/_4$in (6.4mm) diameter, in shades of blue, or white
* ❀ Small round stamens
* ❀ Green covered wire
* ❀ Aquarium greenery, or handmade leaves

FLOWERS

Use the office-style hole punch to cut the circles, as you will need lots of them. For variations in colour, paint the centre of the florets white, pinkish mauve, or a very deep shade of blue – almost navy – before using. Make florets as shown on page 36, but, instead of using a pointed tool, use a very small ball-ended tool or the round end of a small paintbrush so that the florets are a deeply dished shape. You will need quite a large number for each flower spike – anything up to 50 or more.

BUDS

Make some part-opened and some closed buds, but using ¹/₄in (6.4mm) circles of coloured paper and small round stamens (see page 35).

ASSEMBLY

Glue a bud at one end of a 6in (152mm) length of green covered wire. Work down the stem, sticking buds and then florets around the wire stem to form a flower spike with 3in (76mm) to 4in (102mm) of flowers and buds.

Select suitable aquarium green to form a bunch for the base plant about 2in (51mm) high, and stick the flower-spike stems through this into the flowerbed. If you want to make your own leaves, a pattern is given opposite. Use this only as a guide, because the leaves should not be all the same size, and you will probably also need to stick a very fine green covered wire to the back of each leaf.

Note the unopened buds at the tops of these delphinium stems. Delphiniums are seen to advantage in the Cottage Garden, pages 126–7.

Delphinium leaf pattern.

LARKSPUR

The flowers which are sometimes referred to as larkspur are annual delphiniums. Apart from the fact that they are not usually as tall, and are available in a wider variety of colours, they are the same as delphiniums. I use white, mauve, blue, and different shades of pink tissue or paper napkins. The flower spikes should be only 1¹/₂in (38.1mm) to 2in (51mm) long on stems about 2¹/₂in (63.5mm) to 3in (76mm) long, with basal greenery similar to delphinium but only about 1¹/₂in (38.1mm) high, and with smaller leaves.

NASTURTIUM

MATERIALS

- ❀ Yellow, cream, orange, or dark red crepe paper or napkins, cut into circles of about ⁵/₁₆in (7.9mm) to ³/₈in (9.5mm)
- ❀ Covered wire
- ❀ ³/₁₆in (4.8mm) to ⁵/₁₆in (7.9mm) diameter green paper circles
- ❀ Oval stamens, medium-sized

Flowers

The centre parts of the circles can be coloured with felt-tip pens to give variety: orange or red for the yellow ones, red or brown for the orange ones, and dark brown for the red ones. Use the circle sizes given above to make florets, as described on page 36.

Cut short pieces of fine covered wire, bend a tiny bit at one end of each piece at a right angle, and glue the bent-over portion to the side of a floret, so that the flower and stem form a T. When the glue has dried, spray to fix.

Buds

For part-open buds, use a coloured paper floret. Pierce a hole in the base of the floret and pass the stem of an oval stamen through the hole from the inside of the floret. Add a dab of tacky glue to the stamen and squeeze the sides of the floret to stick to the stamen head. When the glue has dried, the edges of some of the florets can be teased out with a darning needle to give varying degrees of opening to the buds. Spray to fix them in a position similar to the flowers, approximately at right angles to the stem. For closed buds, just use an oval stamen, and cover it with a green paper circle.

Leaves

Use circles of green tissue $^3/_{16}$in (4.8mm) to $^5/_{16}$in (7.9mm) in diameter. Cut short lengths, about $^1/_2$in (12.7mm) to $^3/_4$in (19.1mm), of very thin-gauge covered wire and bend about $^1/_8$in (3.2mm) of each end at an angle. Dip this bent part into tacky glue and attach it to the middle of a green circle, then set aside to dry.

Assembly

Cut about $1^1/_2$in (38.1mm) to $2^1/_2$in (63.5mm) lengths of thicker-gauge covered wire. Bend one end at an angle, as for the leaves, and stick one of the smallest green circles to this for a terminal leaf. Working from the end which already has a leaf attached, glue the leaf, flower, and bud stems to the main stem at intervals, bending the stems as necessary. Use the largest leaves last, to finish about 1in (25mm) from the bottom of the stem. Make sure that all the flowers on one main stem are the same colour. Set aside to dry. Repeat to form a number of stems with buds, flowers, and leaves. These can be grouped together to form a wonderful display of trailing nasturtiums. Bunch the stems together, and wind florists' stem tape tightly around the bottom of the stems to keep them together.

For a low-growing clump of nasturtiums, make floret flowers as above, but just stick them to a clump of reindeer moss, as for petunias (below). Nasturtiums are shown in the wooden tub on page 93, and the raised bed on page 90.

PETUNIA

MATERIALS

❀ Tissue paper, crepe paper, or napkins, cut into circles of $^5/_{16}$in (7.9mm) to $^7/_{16}$in (11.1mm) diameter
❀ Green covered wire
❀ Aquarium greenery or dark green reindeer moss

FLOWERS

Colours vary greatly: pink, red, purple, mauve, and white, some having different-coloured centres. The candy-striped ones you sometimes see nowadays were novelties in the Victorian era, so bear this in mind if you are aiming for an authentic 'period' garden. Felt-tip pens can be used to give some circles different-coloured centres: either darker centres of a similar colour, or pink or mauve centres on white circles.

Make petunia flowers by forming the coloured circles into florets (see page 36). The shape can be improved by 'belling' slightly: hold the base of the floret tightly together and press the open end lightly with a finger to open it out a bit.

A colourful display of petunias; for the egg-carton pot, see page 177.

ASSEMBLY

Cut covered wire stems about 1in (25mm) long, apply a dab of tacky glue to the base of a flower, and stick the flower on the end of a stem. Use either small-leafed aquarium greenery or clumps of dark green reindeer moss, the ends of the flower stems being stuck to aquarium greenery with a suitable glue, or dipped in tacky glue and simply pushed into the clump of reindeer moss.

For a mass display on a reindeer moss basis, don't bother with stems. Quite effective results can be obtained by sticking the florets directly on the reindeer moss with a dab of tacky glue, as for the planter in the Patio project (see page 95).

Petunia leaf pattern.

PAPER FLOWERS MADE BY OTHER METHODS

FLAG IRIS

There are many different types of iris flowers, such as the very elaborately coloured, large-flowered garden iris called *bearded iris*, the ones sold in bunches by florists, and the one commonly found growing in, or close to, ponds, which is called a *flag iris*. The latter is quite simple, and is the one described here.

MATERIALS

- ❁ Yellow crepe paper, or recycled yellow fabric flowers
- ❁ Covered wire
- ❁ Grass-like aquarium greenery, or handmade leaves

Full-size pattern for flag iris flower.

FLOWERS

Cut a number of pieces to the pattern given opposite. You will need two for each flower. Pierce a hole in the centre of each, as shown, with a large darning needle. For fabric flowers, paint one side of the fabric with some kind of 'fray-stop' or diluted fabric stiffener and allow it to dry before cutting.

Make a small loop in the end of a piece of covered wire and thread one shaped piece of crepe paper onto this and up to the loop, holding it in place with a touch of tacky glue. These first three petals need to stand upright and curve over towards one another. To curve them, hold the stem so that one of the petals rests on a plastic foam tray, and use a small ball tool. Press it onto the petal and move from the stem towards the outer edge. Curve the other two petals similarly. A spray of hair fix or matt varnish will help to hold them in shape.

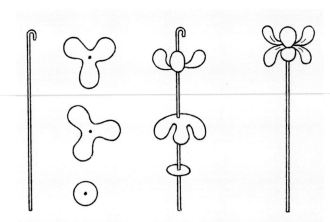

Stages in making the flag iris flower.

The other three petals need to curve downwards, so curve them first, in the same way as for the first three petals, then thread them onto the stem so that they curve down, away from the first three petals, and glue them to the stem as before. Finally, add a circle of green tissue paper about $5/16$in (7.9mm) diameter, threaded onto the stem to within a fraction of the flower. Apply tacky glue, fold the circle in half, roll it around the base of the flower, and use a dab of glue to stick the last bit down.

The simplest material for leaves is aquarium greenery. Choose flat, grass-like leaves, then trim them to length – a bit shorter than the height of the flower stem. Stick two or three of them to the base of the flower stem, trying to keep them flat from back and front, with the flat sides stuck together. Flag irises are shown by the pond on pages 106–7.

Iris leaf pattern.

PANSY

MATERIALS

- ✿ Punched circles of tissue about ¹/₄in (6.4mm) diameter
- ✿ Fine green covered wire (optional)
- ✿ Dark green reindeer moss

FLOWERS

Colour the tissue-paper circles with felt-tip pens to give various combinations of pansy 'faces' (see below). Dish the circles, using a medium round-ended tool or the end of a paintbrush handle (see page 34). The flowers can now be stuck to fine green covered wire in a similar way to the nasturtium leaves above (see page 50), or stuck directly onto the reindeer moss, as in the Patio project (page 95). The effect of the finished flowers benefits from the addition of minute dots of white or pale yellow acrylic paint for the flower centres, as shown in the planter on page 95.

This pansy has handmade paper leaves.

Full-size examples of pansy 'faces'.

ASSEMBLY

Select small clumps of dark green reindeer moss for the basis of the plant. The flowers are stuck to this in groups, with or without stems. You may find it easier to handle the plants if the reindeer moss is glued in position before the flowers are added. Alternatively, make paper leaves to the pattern given.

Pansy leaf pattern.

THREAD FLOWERS

CHRYSANTHEMUMS

Chrysanthemums come in all sorts of sizes and flower types. These are intended to be potentially prize-winning ones, so are fairly large, about $\frac{1}{2}$in (12.7mm) diameter. Smaller flowers for other types of chrysanthemum could be made using the basic method for daisy-like flowers (see page 36).

MATERIALS

- ❀ Crochet cotton or stranded embroidery thread
- ❀ Medium-gauge stem wire about 4in (102mm) long
- ❀ Green paper and/or aquarium greenery

Just some of the many flowers that can be made by the thread method.

FLOWERS

Make flowers using the basic method described on pages 36–7. You will need at least 30 turns of crochet cotton, depending on the thickness, for a nice full flower: if you use embroidery thread, 8 to 10 turns should be sufficient. After the loops of thread have been cut, shape for the particular type of flower you want. I use Humbrol matt varnish in a mini-spraycan to shape and arrange the flowers in two different ways **(remember the safety suggestions for working with sprays, page 11)**. For both, I trimmed the cotton to make the petals shorter at the centre of the flower.

Incurved type: Give a quick burst of spray to one section at a time and, starting with the centre, roll the damp cotton around a cocktail or kebab stick, rolling from the top of the flower and towards the centre; work gradually round and outwards so that all the flower petals are made to curve upwards.

Outcurved or *reflex* type: Spray the centre of the flower and gather together a very small central tuft of petals so that the ends stick together. Let this dry. Shape the rest of the petals as for the first type, except that the cocktail stick or kebab stick is placed *under* the section of damp cotton, and the petals rolled *away* from the flower centre, so that they end up slightly curved *downwards*.

When all is dry, trim the central tuft, and other petals as necessary to give a nice shape to the flower.

LEAVES

Cut tiny scraps of green paper and glue them down the flower stem at intervals for leaves. The shape is given opposite, but as the leaves only want to be ³/₁₆in (4.8mm) to ⁵/₁₆in (7.9mm) in length at the most, this is very fiddly and time-consuming – though very effective. The alternative is to use fairly dark green aquarium plant mat with suitable leaves, or leaves which can be trimmed to a suitable shape.

Chrysanthemum leaf pattern.

ASSEMBLY

For single-stem plants, simply stick the flower stems into the flowerbed. For a larger plant, make three or four stems with just leaves, and bunch these together with two or three flower stems, holding them together by binding the bottoms of the stems with florists' flower-stem tape before planting.

DAHLIA

MATERIALS

- ❁ Crochet cotton or stranded embroidery thread
- ❁ Medium-gauge stem wire, up to 4in (102mm) long
- ❁ Aquarium grass mat, or handmade leaves

FLOWERS

These instructions can be used to make 'cactus'-type dahlia flowers with spiky petals, or 'decorative' type, either large or small. Make the flowers as given above for reflex-type chrysanthemums, varying the size of stick used and the number of turns of thread to make flowers of different sizes. For the 'cactus' type, stick the central tuft together and arrange the petals to form a fairly flat, spiky flower. For decorative types, don't stick the central tuft, and arrange to give a smooth outline, somewhat flatter than a chrysanthemum.

Dahlia leaf pattern.

LEAVES

Aquarium grass mat with oval leaves is the simplest way of making a dahlia plant, but for handmade leaves a pattern is given opposite.

ASSEMBLY

Create bushy-shaped plants varying in height from 1½in (38.1mm) to 3in (76mm), depending on the size of the dahlia flowers, by trimming aquarium greenery as necessary, or using covered wire stems with handmade leaves glued on.

The flower stems should be stuck into the flowerbed to protrude above the greenery, and give a total height of between 2in (51mm) and 4in (102mm).

Dahlias can be seen in the Cottage Garden on pages 126–7.

CARNATION

MATERIALS

❀ Stranded embroidery thread
❀ Medium-gauge stem wire
❀ Plastic Christmas-tree branches, or aquarium plant leaf

FLOWERS

Make the flowers as described in the basic instructions on pages 36–7, but wind the short end of wire further up the threads to keep them bunched closely. You will need about 10 or 12 turns of thread. Trim the ends of the cotton, spray to keep the thread ends in position, and when dry give a final trim.

LEAVES

Plastic greyish-green Christmas-tree branches cut into tiny bits serve well for the greyish spiky leaves of carnations. I simply cut them off, bunch them together, and stick the flower stems in between. An alternative is to use an aquarium plant leaf. Choose one which is fairly broad and cut it across so that you are left with a piece about 1¼in (31.8mm) long. Make cuts down the length of the leaf from the cut end, as closely together as possible, so that there is just a little plastic left holding all the bits together. Use a number of these to form a clump and stick the flower stems in between.

Carnations are shown in the left-hand border of the Cottage Garden on page 126.

ASTER

MATERIALS

❁ Stranded embroidery thread or crochet cotton: white, various shades of pink, and purple; those which are shaded are quite effective
❁ Covered wire
❁ Dark green paper, fabric, or aquarium greenery for leaves

Asters make a fine display as cut flowers; to make the metal pail, see pages 166–7.

FLOWERS

Aster flowers are made in the same way as dahlias (see page 55 above), but the flowers are generally smaller – about ³/₈in (9.5mm) diameter at most.

BUDS

Make partly open flower buds as for carnation flowers (see above).

LEAVES

For handmade leaves, use the pattern opposite, and cut a number of leaves to shape, but of varying sizes. Dish them slightly lengthways, using a ball tool to press the leaf into thin foam and drawing the tool down the length of the leaf.

Aster leaf pattern.

ASSEMBLY

Glue leaves at intervals down the flower stems and bud stems. Make a few stems with just leaves stuck to covered wire. Form a bushy plant by bunching together a number of flower, bud, and leaf stems. Bind the bottoms of the stems together tightly with stem tape. Alternatively, use aquarium plant mat greenery for the bushy basis for the plants, and stick the flower and bud stems through this.

Daisy-like Flowers

There are many daisy-like flowers of various sizes, heights, and colours which can be made using the basic thread flower method (see pages 36–7), but they will probably need fewer turns of thread than larger flowers like chrysanthemums or dahlias.

Experiment with different types of thread, and various numbers of turns, to give you the size you want. Provided that the flower has roughly the right number of petals, the diameter can be trimmed down to size with sharp scissors. This is actually easier, I find, after the flower has been fixed with varnish and the petals are stiff. A dab of thick acrylic paint of the appropriate colour applied to the middle, will serve both for the flower centre and to hide the wire. For example, for pyrethrums, use pink or deep red crochet cotton for the petals and add a yellow centre; for rudbeckia, use yellow for the petals and add a dark brown centre.

You will need to assemble the plant with either suitable aquarium greenery, or handmade leaves to suit the chosen type of flower. A look in a good garden book or catalogue should help to get the right shape of leaf. You will also find many other daisy-like flowers which can be made in a similar way.

PART 2: PROJECTS
SAFETY

Before you start working on any of the projects, please do read the list that follows. Making miniature gardens may seem like a harmless and hazard-free hobby, and some of the things listed here may seem almost too obvious to mention, but following a few simple rules can save no end of heartache. Never forget safety.

BASIC SAFETY RULES

- Any tool can be a potential danger if not stored and handled properly. To avoid nasty accidents, always make sure that tools are kept out of the reach of children at all times.
- All materials are potentially dangerous if misused or if they get into the wrong hands. Many of the materials used in this hobby are attractive to look at, so keep them away from young children.
- Both cleanliness and tidiness are essential for safety. Don't try to work with tools in a cluttered area; you are much more likely to cut something wrongly, or worse still, cut yourself.
- After working, always wash your hands thoroughly before eating or putting your fingers in your mouth – you don't know what may be on them from some of the materials used, or what damage this could do.
- Never smoke whilst working. There is always a fire risk, and material can be transferred from your fingers to a cigarette and thence to your mouth.
- Work in a good light (see page 18), not ordinary room light. It is much easier to cut yourself if you can't see what you are doing properly!
- Always follow manufacturers' and suppliers' instructions for the use and storage of all materials and equipment.
- Make sure that all electrical equipment is wired correctly, has the correct value fuse fitted, and that the supply cable is not damaged in any way. If in doubt consult a qualified electrician.
- Protect your lungs from sanding dust and paint spray by wearing a face mask.
- Keep magnifiers covered and out of the direct rays from the sun in case you start a fire.

LAST WORDS BEFORE YOU BEGIN

Please keep safety in mind at all times. Don't rush; work with care, thoroughness, and patience – this is safest, and leads to the most satisfactory end result.

CHAPTER 9

TRELLIS ARCH

This first complete project can be accomplished using only a craft knife, metal rule, pencil, set square, and scissors, if the instructions are followed carefully. A high-quality job will, however, be made much easier if additional equipment is available, such as a razor saw and mitre block. This will also enable a seat to be made from harder wood, such as obeche or oak.

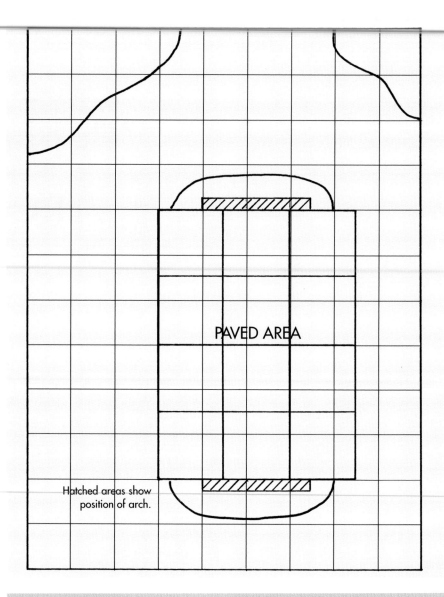

PAVED AREA

Hatched areas show
position of arch.

*Ground plan of the
Trellis Arch garden.*

MATERIALS

- ❁ Baseboard: 9mm (³/₈in) MDF, 12 x 9in (305 x 229mm)
- ❁ Balsa wood, ¼in (6.4mm) square or ¼in (6.4mm) sheet; ¹/₁₆in (1.6mm) sheet
- ❁ Craft felt, green
- ❁ PVA or wood glue
- ❁ Air-drying clay or Dri-Hard
- ❁ Dried flower materials: sea lavender, gypsophila
- ❁ Reindeer moss
- ❁ Paints
- ❁ Wood stain
- ❁ Tacky glue
- ❁ Thick card
- ❁ Thin card

BASEBOARD

The ground plan is not printed full size, so you will need to enlarge it before transferring the plan to the craft felt. Instructions for this are given on pages 24–6.

GRASS

Cut the craft felt to fit the baseboard, and mark out the areas for the flower beds and paving, preferably on what will be on the 'wrong' side (see page 25). Carefully cut around these areas, a little inside the lines to give you a bit of latitude, and remove them. Lay the felt on the baseboard and check that the cut-out areas are correct, then set the felt aside safely, to be fixed later.

PAVING STONES

1   Cut thick card to the size of the area shown on the drawing, 6 x 4¹⁄₂in (152 x 114.3mm), for the paved area. Using a steel rule and an awl, or other pointed implement, mark out evenly spaced paving slabs on the top, by scoring carefully along the side of the rule. Scale size for this paving is approximately 1¹⁄₂in (38.1mm) square. An alternative is to make individual stones from separate pieces of card, as described on page 89.

2   Either Humbrol matt model paint, or colour-match tins of exterior household paint, such as Sandtex, will give very good results. Paint the whole area a suitable stone colour and allow to dry. To give a 'weathered' look, use very much diluted acrylic paint of a darker, brownish-green shade, and go over the first coat of paint again. While this is still wet, dab with a piece of scrunched-up kitchen roll, or a paper tissue, to give a random mottled effect. When the paint is dry, glue the completed paved area to the baseboard in the position marked.

The small bush is made from pink sea lavender.

FLOWERBEDS

Form flower beds with Dri-Hard or air-drying modelling clay, within the areas marked for them on the baseboard. The corner ones should be about ¹⁄₂in (12.7mm) thick in the centre and taper down towards the edges, which should be only about ³⁄₁₆in (4.8mm) thick.

Those at the foot of the arch should slope similarly, from the arch to the outer edges. When they have dried, fix them firmly to the baseboard with PVA glue. The clay can be painted with a 'dirty brown' mixture of brown and green acrylic model paint to simulate the colour of soil.

Oasis or other styrofoam material could be used instead of the air-drying clay; I now use Oasis almost exclusively.

FIXING THE GRASS

Check that the felt grass fits the area left, and trim if necessary. Apply PVA glue to the baseboard area to be covered by the grass – then carefully press the felt smoothly and firmly into position.

TRELLIS ARCH

1 Either buy ready-prepared wood strip of the right size, or cut your own. To do this, use a metal rule as a cutting guide, and make sure that the craft knife blade is held at exactly 90° to the top surface. Cut strips of balsa wood to finish $\frac{1}{4}$in (6.4mm) square. (Similar-sized hardwood section is an alternative, if you have suitable tools to cut it with.)

CUTTING LIST

❀ Uprights	6$\frac{1}{2}$in	(165.1mm)	cut 4
❀ Top pieces	6$\frac{1}{2}$in	(165.1mm)	cut 2
❀ Cross pieces	2in	(51mm)	cut 7
❀ Corner braces	1$\frac{1}{2}$in	(38.1mm)	cut 4

If you cut a little oversize, the pieces can be sanded to size on a sheet of wet-and-dry paper on a sanding board.

2 The uprights will each need cutting at one end for a halved joint. This involves removing a section the same width as the material, and half the depth of the material. The top pieces need cutting similarly for a halved joint at both ends, making sure that the cut-away portions are both on the same face of the square wood. The ends of the four corner braces need cutting at 45° in opposite directions. A small mitre box and razor saw will make this operation much easier and more accurate.

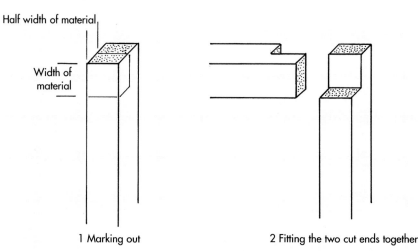

Half width of material

Width of material

1 Marking out

2 Fitting the two cut ends together

Making halved joints.

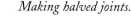

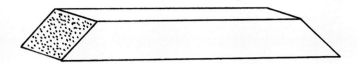

Corner brace with ends cut at 45°.

3 Now is the time to stain each piece, before you start the assembly. Otherwise any glue on the surface will block the stain, and you will have light-coloured patches on the finished article. Apply the stain according to the manufacturer's instructions (I used Colron walnut stain), and leave until thoroughly dry before trying to glue the pieces together.

4 Carefully assemble two uprights and one top piece to form the frame for the front of the arch, and glue the halved joints together, making sure that the whole is squarely lined up. The squaring jig on page 27 is ideal for this; otherwise, use a set square to check your assembly.

   If you have small clamps, these will hold the joints firmly in position until the glue sets: alternatively, use a large rubber band stretched over the joints across the top of the frame. To ensure that the frame stays square, don't move it until the glue is set. Repeat for the back arch frame.

> *A piece of clingfilm on the squaring jig will prevent the assembly from sticking to the jig if there is any excess glue.*

Arch front frame assembled.

5   Glue one of the corner braces across each of the top corners of the front and rear arch frames so that the ends of each one are equidistant from the corner. Use the seven cross pieces to join the front and back frames together. Position one cross piece between each of the bottom and top corners of the two frames, one at the centre of each of the two side frames, and the last one at the centre of the top. (The photographs show an alternative design without the intermediate cross pieces.)

6   From $^1/_{16}$in (1.6mm) thick material cut a number of $^1/_8$in (3.2mm) wide strips. You will need 30 pieces about 4$^1/_2$in (114.3mm) long and 12 pieces about 2$^3/_4$in (69.9mm) long. Stain the strips to match the framework, and allow the stain to dry.

7   Carefully position the strips on one side of the arch frame, glue in place, and leave until the glue is firmly set. Repeat on the other side of the arch, then on the top. Now form the lattice pattern by carefully positioning, then gluing in place, the second layer of strips. Finally, trim the ends of the

Constructing the trellis
(view from above).

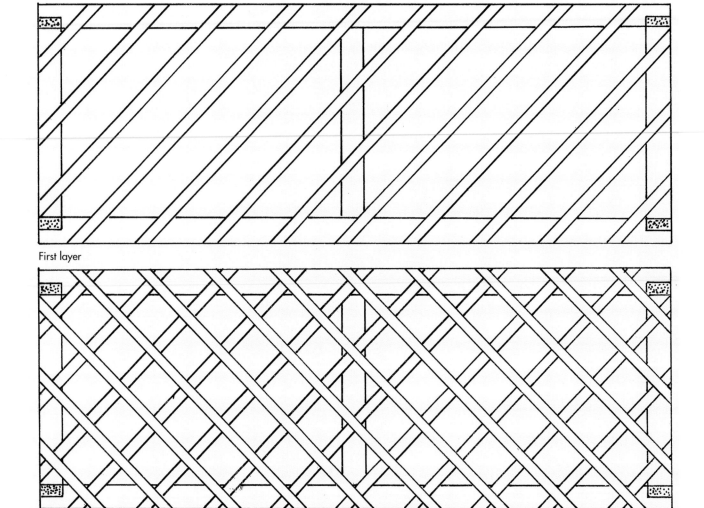

First layer

Second layer

lattice strips in line with the framework. To do this, lay the arch on a firm surface, with the lattice strips downwards, and trim the ends with a sharp knife. Do this for each side and the top. Carefully colour the cut ends of the lattice work to match in with the rest of the arch.

8   The arch can now be fixed to the baseboard, in the position marked on the plan, with PVA wood glue.

CLIMBING ROSE

I used dried plant material with small leaves, which I sprayed green, and dried gypsophila for the flowers.

The trellis with its climbing rose.

1   Select longish pieces of leaf material and, starting at one side of the arch, position the stems and hold them in place by tying neatly with bits of brown sewing thread, and/or with dabs of tacky glue, so that the tops reach about halfway across the top of the arch. Repeat for the other side. If the pieces of plant material are not long enough to reach where you want them, join in extra lengths, by positioning the lower end between an existing stem and the arch, then using a dab of tacky glue to stick the stems together. Let this dry before adding the flowers.

A cocktail stick is useful for applying the glue to the stems, and small crocodile clips or even spring clothes pegs are useful for keeping them together after gluing, and holding them tight until the glue sets.

2 Now thread stems of gypsophila in and through the greenery already attached, apply little dabs of tacky glue where stems coincide, and hold in place until the glue dries. If you are not happy with the result, once the glue has set, extra bits can be added in the same way. An alternative is to make a rambling rose as detailed on page 176.

PLANTS AND FLOWERS

1 Collect together an assortment of small dried plant materials ready to 'plant' your garden, or make plants and flowers of your choice, using the information given in Chapters 6, 7, and 8.

   My arrangement of flowers has purposely been kept simple, and, apart from the climbing rose covering the arch, is restricted to the use of reindeer moss and sea lavender, which can often be bought ready-coloured.

2 For the bush you will need some pink sea lavender. Select two or three pieces about 4in (102mm) long. Apply PVA wood glue to the bottom 2in (51mm) of the stems, and bunch them tightly together. Plastic spring-action clothes pegs can be helpful to hold the bunch tightly until the glue dries. An alternative is to bind the ends of the stems together tightly with florists' stem tape. The bush can then be planted, by making a hole in the clay with an awl or similar implement, and gluing the bottoms of the stems into it with PVA glue.

3 For the flowering plants I used green reindeer moss as the basis. Stick clumps of this to the top of the clay. For taller plants, choose bits of sea lavender about 1¹/₂in (38.1mm) long, either ready-coloured or sprayed with colour to suit your taste. Make holes in the clay, down through the reindeer moss, and glue the flower spikes into them. The shorter plants are smaller bits, about ³/₄in (19.1mm) long, and are just stuck into the reindeer moss with tacky glue.

4 For the smallest plants I sprayed a piece of white sea lavender yellow, and used the individual florets. It is most effective if you keep these in small groups. The easiest way to do this is to put a dab of tacky glue in a foil dish, or on a piece of kitchen foil, pick up a floret with tweezers, dip the bottom of the floret into this to pick up just a tiny touch of glue, then press the floret firmly into the reindeer moss.

EDGING PLANTS

Small pieces of reindeer moss, of varying colours, can now be glued in place on the flowerbeds for edging plants, partly covering some of the edges of the felt grass around them.

GARDEN SEAT

This, like the trellis, is made of balsa wood, or hardwood if you prefer.

For the garden bench, stained balsa gives a convincing imitation of hardwood.

CUTTING LIST

Front legs	A	$1/4$ x $1/4$ x 2in (6.4 x 6.4 x 51mm)	cut 2
Back legs	B	$1/4$ x $1/4$ x $3^1/4$in (6.4 x 6.4 x 82.6mm)	cut 2
Side rails	C	$1/4$ x $1/8$ x $1^1/4$in (6.4 x 3.2 x 31.8mm)	cut 2
Arm supports	D	$1/4$ x $1/8$ x 1in (6.4 x 3.2 x 25mm)	cut 2
Arm rests	E	$3/32$ x $3/8$ x $1^1/2$in (2.4 x 9.5 x 38.1mm)	cut 2
Back rail, upper	F	$1/8$ x $3/8$ x 4in (3.2 x 9.5 x 102mm)	cut 1
Back rail, lower	G	$1/8$ x $1/4$ x 4in (3.2 x 6.4 x 102mm)	cut 1
Back supports	H	$3/32$ x $1/4$ x $7/8$in (2.4 x 6.4 x 22.2mm)	cut 6
Seat rails	I	$1/8$ x $1/4$ x 4in (3.2 x 6.4 x 102mm)	cut 2
Centre seat rail	J	$1/8$ x $1/4$ x $1^1/2$in (3.2 x 6.4 x 38.1mm)	cut 1
Seat bars	K	$3/32$ x $1/4$ x 4in (2.4 x 6.4 x 102mm)	cut 2
		$3/32$ x $1/4$ x $4^1/2$in (2.4 x 6.4 x 114.3mm)	cut 4

Make sure that all ends are cut square (using a mitre box simplifies this procedure), otherwise it will be impossible to glue the seat together properly. Check that the glue has dried thoroughly after each stage before progressing to the next stage.

If you wish to stain the seat, then do so after shaping those pieces which require it, and before starting to glue parts together. Sand each piece very lightly, and remove all dust, before applying the stain or dye in accordance with the manufacturer's instructions. This way you will not get bits where the stain doesn't take well because of the glue. Use a squaring jig to help in assembly, and use clamps or elastic bands to hold bits together until the glue dries.

1 Cut your chosen wood to the sizes given in the cutting list. Take the two back legs (B) and shape one end of each to a radius as shown in the drawing. Form a radius at one end of each of the two arm rests (E) to match the pattern given. The top back rail (F) needs to have one long edge shaped with a radius as shown. These are the only pieces which need shaping, so all the parts can now be stained.

2 Assemble the left-hand seat end frame by taking one back leg (B), one front leg (A), one side rail (C), one arm support (D), and one arm rest (E). Glue them together carefully, checking that all is square. The right-hand seat end frame is the mirror image of the left.

3 The top back rail (F) with the radiused edge, lower back rail (G), and the six back supports (H) are assembled to form the seat back as shown in the drawings. Glue them carefully together, making sure, as before, that everything is square before putting to one side for the glue to set.

4 Take the seat ends, seat back, and the two 4in (102mm) seat rails (I). Carefully glue the seat back in position between the two back legs of the seat ends, one seat rail between the two back legs and one between the two front legs in the positions shown in the drawings, checking for squareness all round. Then glue the centre rail between the two seat rails midway along their length, as shown in the view from underneath. Finally, when the glue has set fully, glue the seat bars or slats in position as shown. The two shorter seat bars are centred over the front and back seat rails, and the others are evenly spaced between.

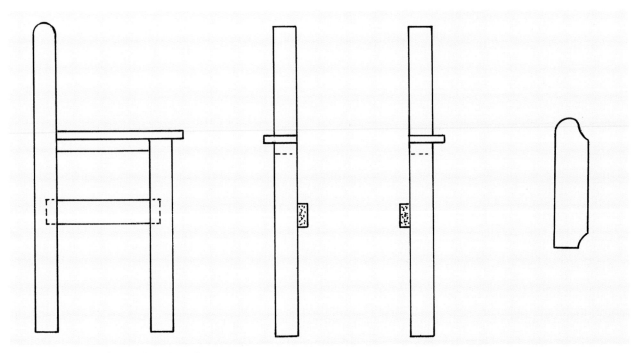

Full-size patterns for bench ends and armrest.

The Dolls' House
Magazine

YOUR INVITATION TO SUBSCRIBE...
VERY SPECIAL OFFER!

e Dolls' House Magazine is a world of miniatures brought to life as ver before. This fascinating magazine is crammed full of projects for u to make and superb examples of the very best work of the world's p miniaturists. Articles are by talented makers, so devoted to their rk that they are happy to share, without reservation, their hard-won crets and experience. Published 10 times a year, *The Dolls' House agazine* is a must for all enthusiasts.

Every issue brings you...

- Dolls' house news from around the world
- Advice and guidance from top makers and authors
- Reviews of all the latest kits and tools
- Lots of projects
- Superb photography

A delicious home

Terry Porter takes time out from editing his own magazine, woodturning, to build this front-opening gable cottage, aptly named Raspberry Parfait Lilliput

INTRODUCTORY OFFER

AVE 20% on a one-year subscription

REE BOOK retail price **£16.95 ($19.95)** on a two-year subscription

BECOME A REGULAR SUBSCRIBER TO

The Dolls' House *Magazine*

TODAY, AND YOU WILL ENJOY...

NEVER MISSING AN ISSUE!
Priority delivery – never miss an issue.

SATISFACTION GUARANTEED!
Guaranteed enjoyment – if you are not 100% satisfied let us know and we will refund the balance of your subscription.

SPECIAL DISCOUNT!
An incredible 20% DISCOUNT on all one-year subscriptions.

FREE BOOK When you take a 2-year subscription.
Receive free, Jean Nisbett's comprehensive book, 'The Complete Dolls' House Book', retail price £16.95 ($19.95).

THE COMPLETE DOLLS' HOUSE ·BOOK·

20% DISCOUNT ~ FREE BOOK

	UK £	US $	OVERSEAS £
12 MONTHS • 10 ISSUES	~~35.95~~ 28.75	~~69.95~~ 55.95	~~42.50~~ 34.00
24 MONTHS • 20 ISSUES	65.00	129.95	75.00
BEST BUY • 2-year subscription includes FREE BOOK! • BEST BUY			

Please send my copies of *The Dolls' House Magazine* to:

Mr/Mrs/Ms ....

Address ....

....

Postcode .... Tel ....

I wish to start my subscription with the month/issue (please complete)

....

CREDIT CARD HOTLINE TEL: 01273 488005 OR FAX 01273 478606

I enclose a cheque to the total value of ☐ £/$

made payable to GMC Publications Ltd.

OR Please debit my credit card* to the value of ☐ £/$

VISA ☐ AMERICAN EXPRESS ☐ ⓘ ☐ MasterCard ☐ SWITCH ☐ *please indicate Switch issue number ☐☐

Account No. ☐☐☐☐☐☐☐☐☐☐☐☐☐☐☐☐☐

Expiry Date ☐☐☐☐ Signature _____

Guild of Master Craftsman Publications will ensure that you are kept up-to-date on other products which will be of interest to you.
If you would prefer not to be informed of future offers, please write to the Marketing Department at the address shown below.

Please post your order to:

Guild of Master Craftsman Publications
Castle Place, 166 High Street, Lewes, East Sussex BN7 1XU England

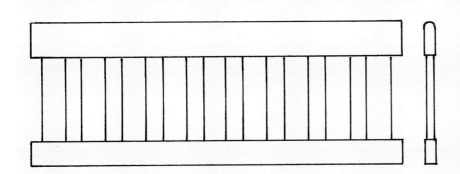

Full-size pattern for seat back.

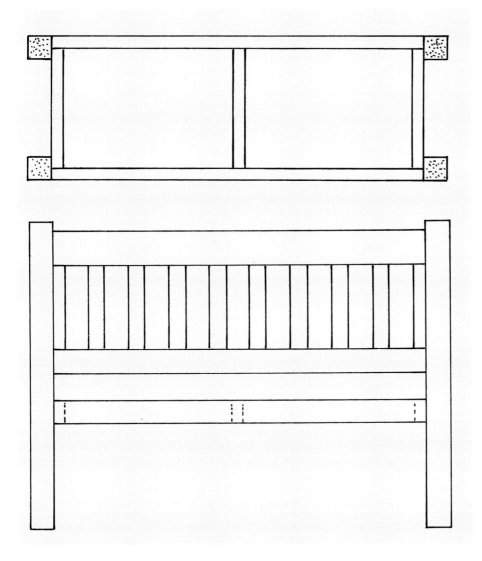

The bench from beneath and from behind, showing positions of seat rails.

5 When all the glue has hardened thoroughly, sand the whole seat very lightly. Remove all the sanding dust and, if you have stained the seat, seal it with a coat of either matt or satin finish acrylic varnish to finish the seat off nicely. An alternative way to finish the seat is by painting it with either model enamel or acrylic paints in whatever colour you want – on

balsa you will first need to use a proprietary grain filler from the DIY store, or the paint will not cover very evenly. Wait until the seat is completely dry before placing it in position.

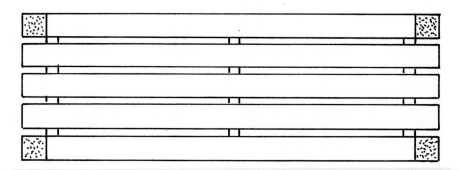

Plan of seat bars, from above.

6 By cutting to the alternative patterns given, variations of the basic seat can be made, assembled in the same way as given above.

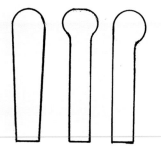

Alternative designs for the seat back and armrests.

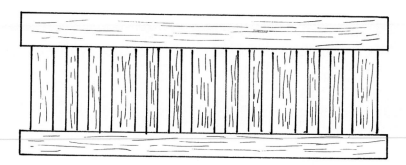

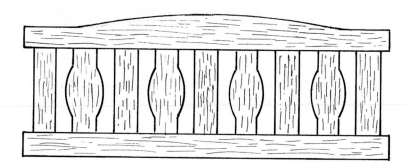

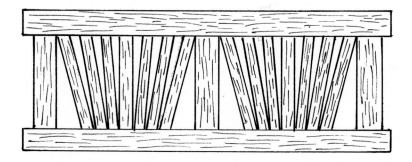

GARDEN TRUG

1 Cut thin card into strips ⅛in (3.2mm) wide. You will need: 3 pieces 5in (127mm) long, 6 pieces 1⅛ (28.6mm), and 3 pieces 1¾in (44.5mm). Trace the layout plan and transfer to a spare piece of paper. Use this as a basis to assemble the strips of card to form the trug.

2 Position the long strip A on the drawing, then position and glue the long strip B to this. Position the short strips D either side of this and glue the bottom ends of them to strip A. Position the long strip C and glue it to the long vertical strip B and the top ends of the short strips D.

3 Now take the remaining three strips E, and thread them through the strips already positioned, weaving them alternately under and over as shown.

4 To form the top edge, wrap each end of the top cross piece C around to cover the ends of the cross strips E and the bottom ends of the short strips D, meeting in the middle of the long strip B, and glue in place. Do not glue the other long strip A in place yet.

5 To form the handle, bend the top end of long strip B over and glue the end over the join where the ends of strip C meet; then bend the bottom end of strip B over and glue it to this, making a double layer. Finally, bend the two ends of long strip A around and glue to long strip C to finish off the top edging and cover all the strip ends.

6 I used buff-coloured card and gave it only a coat of Crystal Clear, but you could paint the whole thing a suitable basket colour with acrylic paint. Fill the trug with 'freshly cut' flowers – select bits of dried flower material, or make flowers as detailed in other chapters.

This delightful trug would look equally at home in any of the other gardens featured in this book.

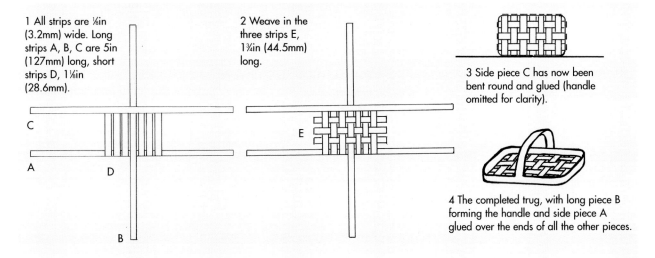

1 All strips are ⅛in (3.2mm) wide. Long strips A, B, C are 5in (127mm) long, short strips D, 1⅛in (28.6mm).

C

A

D

B

2 Weave in the three strips E, 1¾in (44.5mm) long.

E

3 Side piece C has now been bent round and glued (handle omitted for clarity).

4 The completed trug, with long piece B forming the handle and side piece A glued over the ends of all the other pieces.

Stages in making the trug.

CHAPTER 10

WALLED GARDEN

This project demonstrates how Oasis blocks can be used to form stone walling, steps, and flowerbeds, and also introduces an improvised garden pump made from an old felt-tip pen. The plants are kept fairly simple, and show how effective simply made plants can be when massed together.

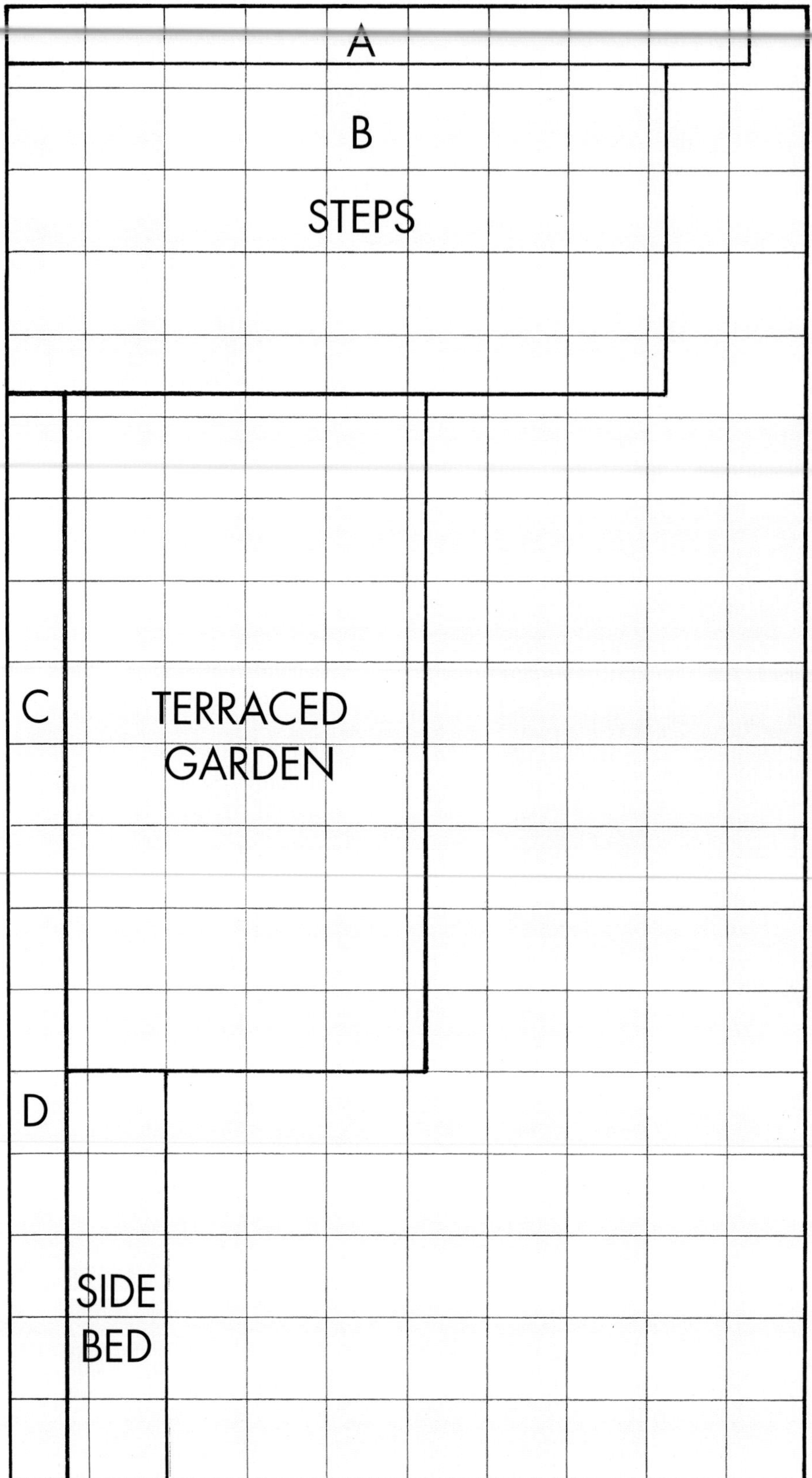

A

B

STEPS

C TERRACED
GARDEN

D

SIDE
BED

E

*Ground plan of the
Walled Garden.*

MATERIALS

- ❀ Baseboard: 9mm ($^3/_8$in) MDF, 19 x 10in (483 x 254mm)
- ❀ Walling: Oasis or Dryfoam rectangular bricks approximately 9 x 4$^1/_4$ x 3in (229 x 108 x 76mm)
- ❀ Acrylic paints
- ❀ Planting: tacky glue, dried flower material, aquarium greenery, reindeer moss, railway layout conical fir tree
- ❀ Pump: old felt-tip pen with a short portion of the cap deeply ridged, wire, beads, paint, card, tiny nails

BASEBOARD

Cut the baseboard to size and transfer the project plan onto it, enlarged using the method described on pages 24–6.

WALLING

1 You need slices of Oasis about $^3/_4$in (19.1mm) thick for the walling around the edge of the garden, so, with the largest face of the brick for the top, mark a line all round the brick $^3/_4$in (19.1mm) down from the top edge. Start cutting from a short end, with the knife blade on the marked line. Carefully cut through the styrofoam, keeping the handle end of the blade on the line marked on one long side, and the point end of the blade on the line on the opposite long side of the brick. Repeat this procedure until you have four slices, sufficient to match the wall area marked on the drawing.

2 Transfer the pattern for the shape of the left-hand wall (E) onto one slice and cut to this shape.

3 From another Oasis brick, cut the steps using the side plan given. Mark this on the two opposite long sides of a brick, and cut between the two sets of markings as detailed above.

4 Cut the stone terraced flowerbed from yet another Oasis brick, following a similar procedure.

5 Position the cut Oasis slabs as shown on the plan. Start with the slab for the right-hand side wall (A), and apply PVA glue to the bottom edge. Position this block carefully and press it firmly onto the baseboard, then leave it to allow the glue to dry.

6 Apply PVA glue to the bottom and right-hand side of the steps (B).

Cutting and detailing blocks of Oasis is a messy job, so a covering of newspaper over the working area is advised. Then all the bits can be gathered up with the paper, and disposed of. Use a long-bladed knife to cut the Oasis bricks to give you slabs for the walls. I used the carving knife, washed it up and put it away again quickly before anyone noticed!

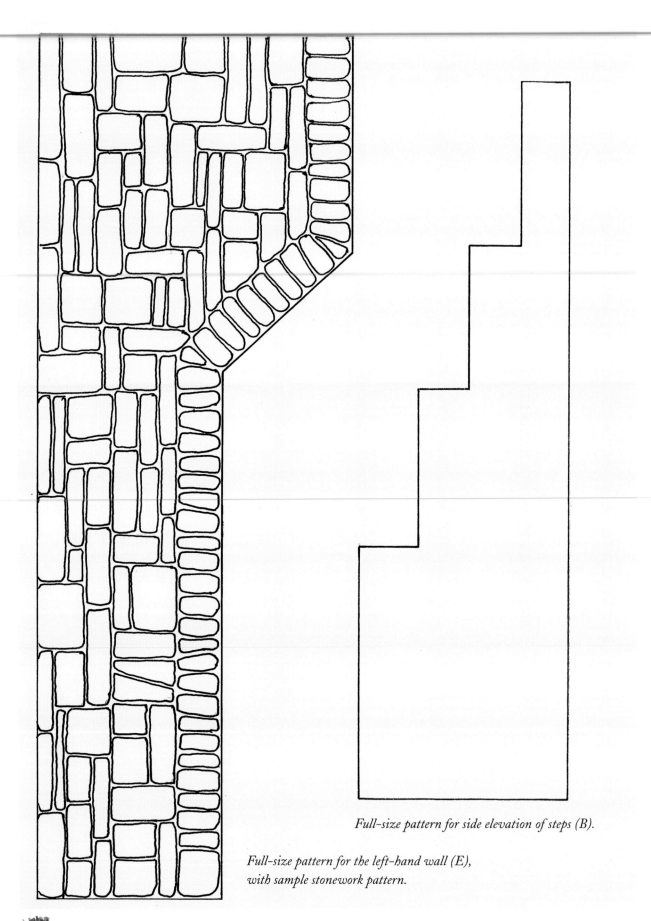

Full-size pattern for side elevation of steps (B).

*Full-size pattern for the left-hand wall (E),
with sample stonework pattern.*

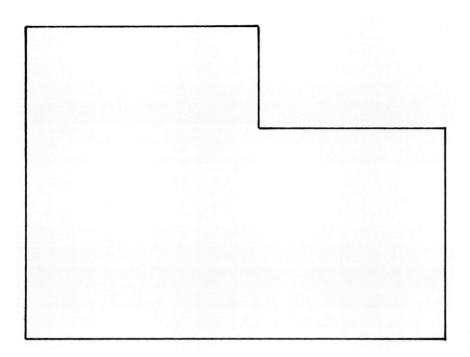

Full-size pattern for ends of terraced beds.

Position them, and press firmly onto the baseboard and the side wall, holding the outside of the right-hand side wall so that it is not pushed out of position.

7   The adjoining back wall (C) is the next one to be glued in place, with PVA glue on the bottom edge and the side where it butts up to the steps. Position this and press firmly in place. Now check the last piece of back wall (D) for length, trimming if necessary. To keep this lined up with the piece already fixed, push a couple of cocktail sticks up to half their length into the end of the block already positioned, to act as dowels.

8   Put PVA glue on the bottom edge of piece D, and the edge which will join up with the other back wall (C). Position this last slab by placing it on the baseboard and pushing sideways, over the cocktail sticks, so that it lines up with the existing back wall, and press firmly into place.

9   The left-hand side wall (E) can be glued into position now, with PVA glue on the bottom edge of the slab and on the portion that butts against piece D. Hold the back wall firmly against the end of it until the glue sets.

10 Finally, apply PVA glue to the back, base, and right-hand side of the terrace block and press this firmly in position until the glue dries. Short pieces of cocktail sticks used as dowels, as before, will give added strength.

11 Using an awl or similar pointed tool, mark the exposed surfaces of the walling for stonework. A sample pattern is included for your guidance in the drawing of the left-hand wall, and the result is shown in close-up in the photographs. Mark stone edgings to the steps in a similar way.

12 Mix a fairly large quantity of acrylic paint of a suitable stone colour. I used Rowney System 3 in yellow ochre, white, brown, and black. Paint all the exposed wall surfaces and the stone step edges. When this is dry, make a very thin mix of a darker, greeny-grey stone colour, and a similar but lighter shade. Go over random patches of the stonework and step edges with these two colours to give a weathered effect. Paint the step treads with an earthy-coloured acrylic paint.

SIDE FLOWERBED

Cut a piece of Oasis about ³/₈in (9.5mm) thick and 1¹/₂in (38.1mm) wide to fit between the end of the terraced beds and the left-hand side wall, sloping the front edge slightly, as for the flower beds in the previous project, and glue in place in the corner.

GRASS

Cover the remaining area with grass material of your choice. I used railway layout scenery mat, the shade called Autumn Green, stuck firmly to the baseboard with PVA glue. Cut the grass material a good inch (25mm) oversize along the front edge, and along the sides as far as the walls. Apply PVA glue to the baseboard area to be covered, and carefully smooth on the grass material, then glue the overlap to the edges and bottom surface of the baseboard, trimming the corners as necessary to give a neat effect.

PLANTING

Collect together and/or make the plant materials you wish to use in the terraced bed. If you just push them gently a little way into the Oasis you will be able to reposition them until you are satisfied with the result, and then glue them in place. My aim here was not to try to imitate any particular flower or plant, but to give an overall colourful mass of flowers, of varying heights, created as simply as possible. I used mostly dried grasses, commercial dried flowers, sea lavender, statice, and dried daisy-like flowers painted with fabric paints, with one or two bushes of aquarium greenery, and a railway layout tree about 7in (178mm) high.

RIGHT-HAND WALL

Selected pieces of dried sea lavender were used for the climbing plant against the right-hand side wall. I bought some already coloured pink. This was trimmed to fit where I wanted it and the stems pushed into the Oasis join between the wall and the steps with some PVA glue, and then secured in place against the wall with tiny dabs of tacky glue. For added security use short pieces of florists' wire, about ³/₄in (19.1mm), bent in half and pushed into the Oasis walling to straddle the plant stem like a staple.

Pink sea lavender makes the climbing plants on the right–hand wall.

TERRACED BEDS

Bunches of aquarium mat with different-shaped leaves were stuck into the Oasis for bushes in front of the back wall, and made to bloom by the addition of bits of dried plants, either stuck to them with tacky glue, or with longer stems pushed down through the leaves into the Oasis. Medium-height plants were made from bits of aquarium plant mat with small leaves. The bases of the plants were stuck into the Oasis, and the stems of dried flowers, coloured with fabric paint, stuck in between them. Low-growing blue and mauve flower clumps were fashioned from bits of dried statice heads glued directly into the Oasis. Sea lavender pieces, some bought in white and some already coloured pink or blue, serve for pieces of sprawling plants. The ends of their stems are stuck into the Oasis at various angles, so that some bits curve, or trail, over the top of the walling. For other trailing plants I chose clumps of purple, orange, and pink reindeer moss with straggly ends. The main clump of each is glued to the Oasis, so that the straggly ends drape over the wall. Small clumps of reindeer moss in all sorts of colours fill the remaining gaps.

The terraced beds are a riot of colour.

SIDE BED

The small side flowerbed has a slender, conical, railway layout tree in one corner. The bottom was trimmed and then glued into the Oasis, and a tall plant made with spiky aquarium plant leaves glued into the Oasis at the other side, with selected pieces of blue-coloured sea lavender stems pushed down through the leaves and stuck into the Oasis. Long slender stems of dried flower material with tiny flowers created the tall plant against the wall, which was attached in the same way as the one on the right-hand wall. Bits of dried statice heads form medium-height and lower clumps of flowers, and are glued into the Oasis. Lumps of bright orange, purple, white, and green reindeer moss are glued to the Oasis to cover the rest of this bed.

This cupressus or juniper tree was originally intended for a model railway layout.

WALL AND STEPS: FINAL TOUCHES

To give the final touches to the walling and steps I used bits of fine green foam scatter material for moss, yellow foam scatter for lichen, and some weeds made of tiny bits of reindeer moss. Use tacky glue to paint small areas of the steps which might be mossy, and press very fine green foam scatter material onto it. Create areas of yellow lichen similarly. Larger pieces of green foam were used on the front of the walling and to the right of the steps; for these, a small dab of tacky glue is applied and then the individual bits of foam pressed onto it. Along the foot of the wall, some of the larger pieces of green foam were first dipped into tacky glue, and then pressed into a little heap of fine yellow railway layout flock material, before being stuck in place to look a bit like stonecrop. Tiny, broken-up bits of reindeer moss are stuck on with tacky glue, some over green foam and some on their own, for weeds and small wall plants.

Look at some old damp walling if you can – it will give you an idea of where patches of moss and lichen are most likely to grow, and also of the often unlikely places in which weeds and other plants manage to grow on walling.

Moss-covered steps give the Walled Garden a well-established look.

PUMP

1 For this I used an ancient felt-tip pen, electric wire, two plastic beads, card, and a short piece of plastic-covered garden wire, to simulate the type of pump which could have been found in almost any cottage garden at one time. The type of pen with a short, deeply ridged portion at the top of the cap works best. Use tweezers to remove any remaining ink material from the pen body casing.

2 Cut a section of casing about 4in (102mm) long and glue the pen top firmly back onto this. Then cut a ³/₄in (19.1mm) square piece of plastic or cardboard for the base, and glue the pen firmly to the centre of this, with the cap uppermost, making sure that it is absolutely vertical.

3 For the spout, cut a piece of insulated single-core electric wire about 1in (25mm) long and ¹/₈in (3.2mm) in diameter, and remove the plastic insulation from about ¹/₄in (6.4mm) of it. Make a hole in the pump, push the bared end of wire into the hole, and use pliers to bend the plastic-covered portion of the wire to form a spout shape, then glue it firmly in position.

4 Use the pattern to cut two pieces of thin card or plastic, and shape a piece of thin plastic-coated garden wire (about ¹/₁₆in (1.6mm) in diameter) for the handle. Sandwich the top end of the handle between the two shaped pieces of plastic or card and glue them firmly together. Finish off the handle by attaching a small plastic bead to the lower end. When the glue has dried thoroughly, attach the handle assembly to the pump by pushing the shaped top portion firmly between two ridges on the pump head, at 90° to the spout, and glue in place.

5 Finish the whole thing off with a plastic bead stuck to the top of the pump.

6 After all the glue has dried thoroughly, the pump can be painted. I used aluminium spray paint; it would also look good in dark green.

7 When the paint is dry, the pump can be fixed in the chosen position. Mark the grass around the base of the pump, remove the pump, and scrape away the grass within the area marked. Glue the pump in place, and knock in a tiny nail at each corner of the base to represent bolts. Finally, cover the nail heads with dabs of paint to blend them in with the rest of the pump.

8 The area around the base of the pump could be 'landscaped' a little with tacky glue, flock material, and tiny bits of reindeer moss as given for the steps and walling above.

The old cast-iron water pump was once a felt-tip pen.

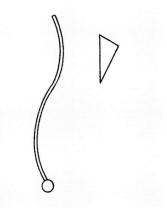

Full-size patterns for pump handle and bracket.

CHAPTER 11

PATIO GARDEN

Here you can create a superbly colourful display of plants and flowers in containers of all sorts: planters, tubs, pots, a sink garden; with a raised brick flowerbed and a basket chair from which to view the whole display.

Do make absolutely sure that
any bottle or container tops are
well and truly washed out
before using them in your
garden scheme.

A good source of suitable containers for your plant pots is possibly under the
kitchen sink! The tops of many common household cleaners make ideal
containers when painted a suitable colour, turned upside down, and 'planted' to
your choice. Accumulate a selection of different shapes and sizes.

Many florists now sell tiny terracotta pots, some of which are about the
right size to be used with 1/12 scale, particularly for shrubs and larger
plants. Don't forget that even a very large plant pot of 15in (381mm)
diameter will only be 1¼in (31.8mm) across when scaled down to 1/12 size!

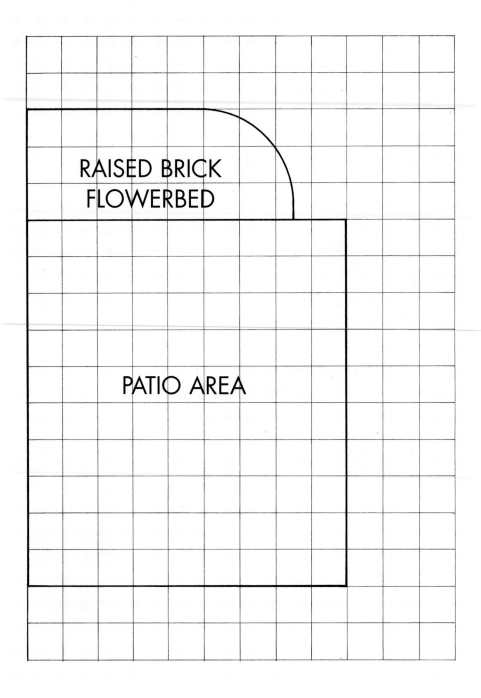

*Ground plan for the
Patio Garden.*

MATERIALS

- ❀ Baseboard: 9mm (³⁄₈in) MDF, 17 x 12in (432 x 305mm)
- ❀ Very thick card, 10 x 9in (254 x 229mm)
- ❀ Rectangular block of Oasis or similar
- ❀ Acrylic paints, varnish
- ❀ Sample tin of textured exterior paint, such as Sandtex
- ❀ Air-drying clay, terracotta and white
- ❀ Bottle tops
- ❀ Terracotta pots
- ❀ Railway layout dark brown ballast
- ❀ Thin card (an old greetings card is ideal)
- ❀ Fablon or similar green self-adhesive velour, or railway layout grass mat material
- ❀ PVA glue
- ❀ Plant materials of your choice, or handmade flowers
- ❀ Plastic-covered electric wire (or garden wire), about ¹⁄₈ and ³⁄₃₂in (3.2 and 2.4mm) thick
- ❀ Buttonhole thread
- ❀ Aida (or similar) cross-stitch material, 14-count
- ❀ Crochet cotton, no. 20

BASEBOARD

Enlarge the plan as detailed on pages 24–6, and transfer it to the baseboard.

PAVING

1   Using a steel ruler as a straightedge to cut along, measure and cut the cardboard to the following sizes for paving stones (the metric conversions have been rounded down to enable the pieces to interlock accurately):

2 x 2in	(50 x 50mm)	cut 7
2 x 1in	(50 x 25mm)	cut 20
1 x 1in	(25 x 25mm)	cut 22

2   Paint the paving stones with Sandtex, or a similar fine-textured exterior paint (sample tins are available from DIY superstores). When the paint is dry, glue the paving in position on the baseboard as in the plan. Give it a slightly weathered appearance by going over some areas with a watery mix of acrylic paint of a dirty greenish-brown colour. Dabbing with a paper tissue will help give a random effect and remove excess paint.

*Full-size plan of
the patio paving.*

*A view of the raised
brick flowerbed.*

RAISED FLOWERBED

1   Using a long-bladed knife, cut a rectangular Oasis brick to the size and
    shape given by the *outer* line in the plan (see page 77 for the technique).
    Make sure that the cut is absolutely vertical.

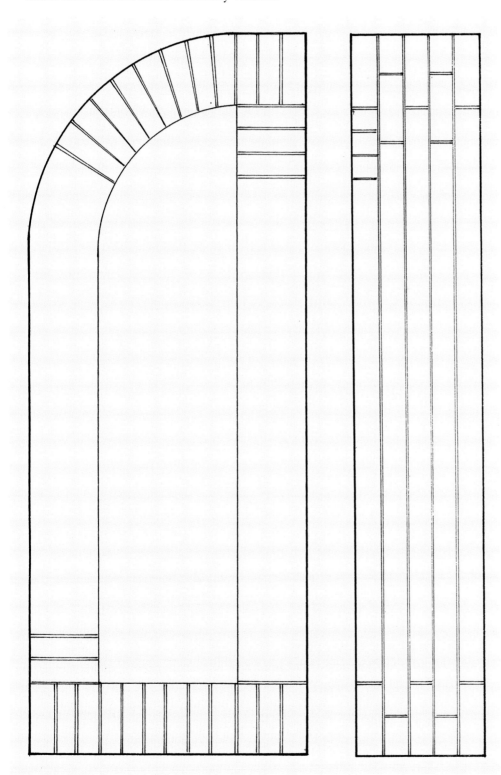

*Full-size plan and
side elevation of the
raised brick bed.*

Mark out the top area from the pattern, then cut vertically to a depth of about ¹/₂in (12.7mm) along the *inner* line, which will be the inside of the walling. Now cut at a shallow angle from about ¹/₄in (6.4mm) inside this, towards the wall, and remove the wedge-shaped part to give a slope to the soil inside your raised bed.

2 Use an awl, cocktail stick, or similar implement to mark the brickwork. First mark a line all round the Oasis about ³/₈in (9.5mm) down from the top edge. This will be the bottom of the edging bricks and the top of the side wall brick courses.

   The top edging bricks of the walling should be marked about ¹/₄in (6.4mm) apart to simulate a brick-on-edge top to the walling. A sample of this is shown in the drawing. The markings should be carried vertically down the sides of the walling to the line previously marked.

   The remainder of the walling should be marked out for courses of brickwork.

3 I used Humbrol matt acrylic paint for my brickwork. Mix a fairly large quantity of brownish-red, and paint the bricks with this. When this is dry, mix various shades of brown and green to a very thin, watery consistency, and go over the first coat in random patches, to give the bricks a weathered look. Paint the garden area in the top, with a dirty brown earth colour. When all the paint is dry, use PVA glue to stick the completed raised brick bed to the baseboard, in the position marked on the layout plan.

GRASS SURROUND

Mark the back of the self-adhesive velour (or other material) for the remaining area, around the paving and the raised brick bed, allowing an extra 1in (25mm) on the baseboard edges, then cut the central area out with sharp scissors. Remove the backing from the self-adhesive material little by little, and press it firmly onto the baseboard, smoothing as you go, to exclude air bubbles. Turn the excess over the edges of the baseboard, and use PVA glue to stick it firmly to the bottom of the board.

PLANTING THE RAISED BRICK BED

You can use whatever planting you choose for the raised brick bed, to make it as simple or as detailed as you like, using the information and ideas from earlier chapters. For my planting I chose to have one of the bushes made from sea lavender, as in the Trellis Arch project (see pages 63 and 68), but this time using white sea lavender; the other was a rose bush (see page 42), using yellow paper for the roses, and a piece of aquarium mat greenery for the bush. I also used reindeer moss, and petunia, begonia, and nasturtiums

WOODEN TUB

1   You will need a piece of thin card about 9 x 3in (229 x 76mm) as the basis, cut to the pattern shown. Cut $^1/_{16}$in (1.6mm) balsa wood into strips about $^1/_4$in (6.4mm) wide, tapered slightly as shown, to fit the card pattern. You will need about 30 strips, $1^3/_4$in (44.5mm) long.

2   Stain the strips a fairly dark colour; I used Colron walnut stain.

3   When dry, use PVA glue to stick the strips of wood to the card pattern, trimming where necessary. A weight placed on top will stop the pieces distorting as the glue dries. When the glue has dried completely, roll up the whole thing, with the wood to the outside, and glue the overlap tab inside the tub, holding the joint firmly in place until the glue sets. Spring clothes pegs are handy for this.

The wooden tub is planted with roses, nasturtiums, and begonias.

4   Cut a circle of balsa for the base, apply PVA glue to the bottom $^1/_4$in (6.4mm) of the card, inside the wooden tub surround just made, and push the circle of balsa down into place from the top to wedge it firmly and squarely inside. Hold the tub surround tightly to the balsa base so that it sticks firmly to the cardboard; a wide rubber band is useful for this.

5   Cut three $^3/_{16}$in (4.8mm) wide strips of thin card sufficiently long to wrap once around the wooden cladding and overlap about $^1/_2$in (12.7mm): one about $^3/_8$in (9.5mm) from the top, one about $^1/_4$in (6.4mm) up from the bottom, and another one the same distance above this. Paint the card strips, apart from the bit that will be overlapped, with a dirty matt black colour and allow to dry. Apply tacky glue to the unpainted overlap end of the strips, wrap around the tub, and stick firmly in place to simulate iron bands.

Full-size pattern for the wooden tub.

Joining tab

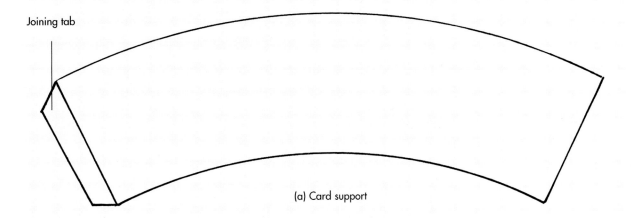

(a) Card support

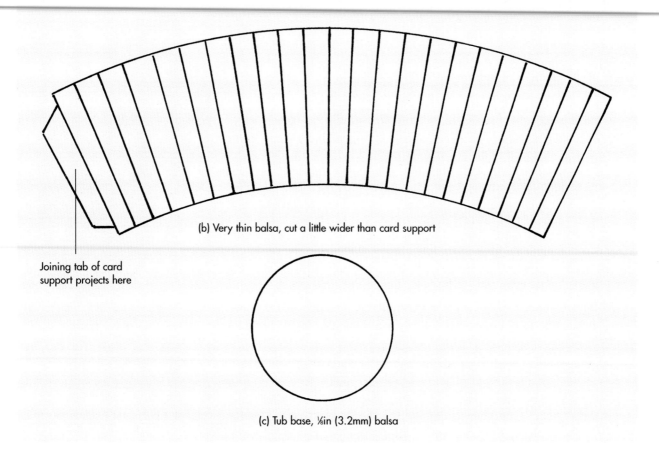

(b) Very thin balsa, cut a little wider than card support

Joining tab of card
support projects here

(c) Tub base, ⅛in (3.2mm) balsa

*Full-size pattern for
the wooden tub.*

PLANTING THE TUB

Select bits of plastic or artificial plant material, dried flowers, and grasses to
plant your tub, or make handmade flowers as described in Chapters 6, 7,
and 8. Use Dri-Hard or similar dried flower base material to half-fill the
tub and give it weight, then cut a piece of Oasis to fit inside the top of the
tub, and stick this to the top of the Dri-Hard and the inside of the tub with
PVA glue. Paint the top of the Oasis with dirty brown acrylic paint for the
soil, and push your selected plants into this.

The planting shown in the photographs is as follows. The rose bush in
the centre (see page 42) is made from a table napkin and plastic aquarium
plant; push the stem into the centre of the Oasis. Nasturtiums (see pages
49–50) in cream, yellow, and dark red are pushed into the Oasis around the
rose bush, using tweezers to arrange the stems so they spread out over the
tub and bend over the edge. Begonias (see page 40), made from deep red,
light red, and yellow tissue paper with leaves cut from an aquarium plant,
are planted in between the stems of the nasturtiums.

Bits of coloured reindeer moss can be glued to the Oasis around the
edge, so that they drape over the side of the tub, and held there with tiny
dabs of tacky glue, to give the finished effect of a full tub with plants
spilling over the edge.

TERRACOTTA PLANTERS

Terracotta planters with pansies (left) and petunias.

1   Use terracotta-coloured Das, or similar air-drying clay, to make the planters. A piece of wood, approximately 3 x 1 x $^7/_8$in (76 x 25 x 22.2mm), will be needed as a former. Wrap the wood in clingfilm to stop the clay sticking to it, and knock a small nail a little way into the centre of the $^7/_8$in (22.2mm) side to give you something to get hold of when you want to get the former out.

2   Using either a round glass bottle or a small rolling pin smoothly covered in clingfilm, and working on a foil-covered board, roll out a piece of Das about $^1/_4$in (6.4mm) thick and large enough to be covered by the piece of wood. Place the base of the former (the side opposite the nail) onto the clay, and carefully cut round to make the base of the planter. Roll out another piece of Das to give a strip a little over 1in (25mm) wide, about 8in (203mm) long, and fairly thin; about $^1/_8$in (3.2mm) is fine. Moisten the edges of the clay base with water and wrap the second strip of clay around the base and the former to make the sides of the planter. Trim the ends to length, moisten with water, and press firmly together to make a good joint where the two ends meet. It is best if this is at a corner. Trim the clay level with the top of the wood. Moisten the surface with a little water as necessary to smooth it with modelling tools to get rid of any finger marks; aim to end up with fairly sharp corners and a smooth top edge.

3   Leave for a little while until the clay starts to harden, then very carefully loosen the wooden former slightly by wiggling it gently, and after a little while longer, remove it altogether. Leave to dry out completely. The reason for removing the former is that the clay shrinks as it dries, so if the former is left in position either the clay will crack, or you won't be able to get the former out, or possibly both! This should give you a planter about 3 x $^7/_8$ x 1in (76 x 22.2 x 25mm). Make another planter similarly.

PLANTING

Glue a piece of Oasis inside each planter for the soil, and paint the top with dirty brown acrylic paint. You can fill your planter with any plants of your choice, by pushing their stems into the Oasis, or by sticking them onto the Oasis with tacky glue.

The ones shown in the photographs were planted using only reindeer moss as a basis, and sticking flowers to this. Some bits of purple reindeer moss were left as they were for plants such as aubrietia and alyssum. Select a few straggly bits of purple or white reindeer moss, and glue one end to the Oasis so that the rest hangs over the edge. Fairly round pieces of green reindeer moss should be stuck on top of the Oasis along the length of the planter.

One of mine has lots of petunia flowers (see page 51); the base of each floret is stuck to the reindeer moss with tacky glue, each group of florets having flowers of just one colouring to indicate separate plants.

The other planter is full of pansies (see page 53), stuck to the reindeer moss with small dabs of tacky glue in clusters, to form mounds of plants along the length of the planter.

SINK GARDEN

The sink garden.

To make a sink garden, follow the same method as for the planter, but use white Das, and a wooden former 2in (51mm) long, 1½in (38.1mm) wide, and ⅝in (15.9mm) deep. When the clay is completely dry, give the surface a rub over with very fine wet-and-dry paper, remove all the dust, and wipe over with a damp cloth to give a really smooth finish. When it is completely dry again, either give the outside a coat of gloss varnish for a glazed white sink or, if you would prefer a stone sink, mix a suitable stone colour with matt acrylic paint, or select a suitable colour of exterior masonry paint. Finally, when the varnish or paint is dry, cut a piece of Oasis to fit, and glue this inside to hold the plants. Simulate soil by painting the top of the Oasis with a dirty brown acrylic paint.

An alternative method of creating a sink garden is to use the bottom of a white plastic tablet container. Make sure that the container is well washed out and the label removed. Draw a pencil line around the container about ⅝in (15.9mm) up from the bottom, then cut along the line with a sharp craft knife. Fill the sink with Das, or similar, to give it some added weight. Either push the plant stems into the clay before it dries; or allow the clay to dry, paint it soil colour, and then make holes for the plants with an awl or something similar; or glue reindeer moss plants on top of the clay.

PLANTING

I chose to plant my sink garden using only dried grasses, aquarium greenery, artificial stamens, and reindeer moss, but you could choose from any of the ideas given in this book. I glued small clumps of reindeer moss in various colours to the top of the clay, with some straggly bits draped over the sides. For ferns, bunch small bits of feathery aquarium leaves together, and bind the bottoms tightly together with fine covered wire, before planting them. Small clumps of green reindeer moss are used as a basis for other plants, with various sizes and colours of artificial stamens, cut to different lengths, for the clumps of small flowers. Put a blob of tacky glue on a piece of foil or in a small foil dish, dip the ends of the stamen stems into this, and push them into the reindeer moss in groups to form mounds of flowers. Small bits of the ubiquitous dried sea lavender, pink, white, and blue, were used for the other plants in my sink garden.

POT PLANTS

Use bought terracotta pots, home-made pots (see page 145), or converted bottle tops to hold your own choice of plants. The ones shown in the photograph are detailed below.

For a specimen shrub I chose a camellia (see page 41), using a terracotta pot about 1in (25mm) in diameter, bought at my local florist's, as the container. Das air-drying clay was pushed into the pot to within $\frac{1}{8}$in (3.2mm) of the top, and the camellia pushed into the centre of this.

Camellia. Note the realistic use of railway layout ballast as compost.

Bottle tops give a convincing representation of modern plant pots.

A selection of differently shaped bottle tops, painted with acrylic or masonry paint, serves for the other plant containers. These are filled with air-drying clay to add weight and stop them toppling over too easily. Some have bits of aquarium greenery stuck into the clay in clumps; some, like the sink garden, have reindeer moss stuck on top of the clay and artificial-stamen flowers. Others have petunias or pansies (see page 53), nasturtiums (see pages 49–50), or double begonias with flowers of various colours (see page 40).

One bought terracotta pot is planted with only a piece of small-leafed aquarium greenery, the edges painted cream for a variegated bush (see page 31); another has a pampas-grass-type plant made from dried grass heads, and leaves cut from thin green card.

To give a really nice finish, the top of the clay holding the plants should be coated with PVA glue, and railway layout fine, dark brown ballast, sprinkled over. Stand the pots on a sheet of paper to do this. When the glue has hardened, blow gently to remove any bits which haven't stuck. Any surplus will then be collected on the sheet of paper, and can be reused.

Pampas grass.

PATIO CHAIR

The one shown is made from plastic-covered electric wire about $\frac{1}{8}$in (3.2mm) and $\frac{3}{32}$in (2.4mm) diameter (thick plastic-covered garden wire could be used instead), with buttonhole-thread binding. The basketwork is simulated by using 14-count Aida cross stitch embroidery material with a plaited crochet-cotton trim.

The patio chair is seen here in the Cottage Garden (see Chapter 13).

1 Form the thicker wire to the patterns given for the outer framework, inner back framework, and seat framework, gluing the ends of the plastic of the seat frame firmly together. Bend the two sides of the outer framework so that they are at right angles to the centre portion, to form

the arms and front legs. Glue the inner back framework inside the outer framework to form the chair back and back legs. Adjust the angle of the chair back and legs, and glue the seat frame in position.

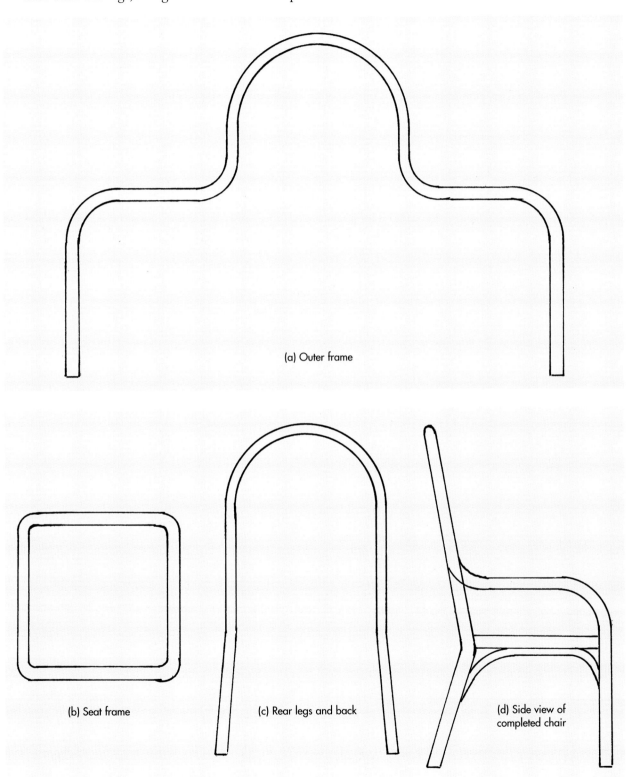

(a) Outer frame

(b) Seat frame

(c) Rear legs and back

(d) Side view of completed chair

Full-size patterns for the patio chair.

2 When the glue has set fully, add thinner pieces of covered wire to make the braces beneath the seat. Use the buttonhole thread to bind tightly over the joints, and secure with PVA glue. Give the plastic a coat of white primer, then, when this is fully dry, a finishing coat of white gloss. Let this harden fully before handling again.

3 Cut a piece of Aida for the basketwork, large enough to fit over the framework and leave some extra for trimming. Coat completely in slightly diluted fabric stiffener, then squeeze out the excess carefully, by rolling in a piece of clean rag or an old towel. Place the damp Aida over the framework of the chair, and carefully shape it to fit neatly. Leave until completely dry – overnight is best. Gently remove the Aida, apply PVA glue to the framework, and replace the Aida. Press it gently but firmly into position and then leave for the glue to dry thoroughly.

Making the plaited trimming for the patio chair. **Note:** *All threads should be the same colour; they are shown here in different colours only so that the three separate strands can be clearly distinguished.*

4 Meanwhile, make the plaited trimming. Cut six lengths of crochet cotton or buttonhole thread about twice as long as is needed to follow the edges of the Aida basketwork. Tie the ends together and fasten to a board with a drawing pin pushed firmly through the knot, then plait, using two strands of cotton together and working alternately left over right, and right over left. Try to keep the tension even and the plait as flat as possible. Tie a spare piece of thread around the ends of the plait to hold them temporarily, until after fixing, so that the plait can be trimmed to length.

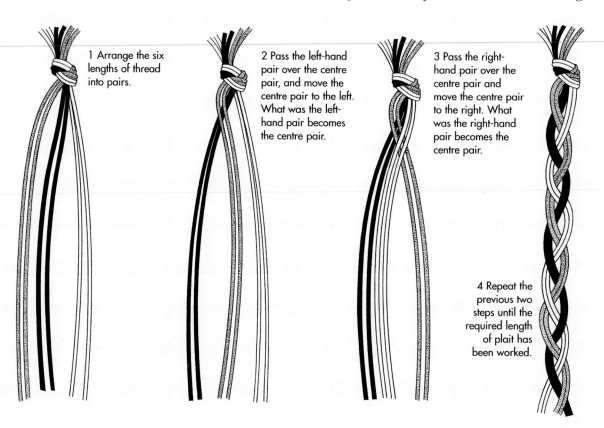

1 Arrange the six lengths of thread into pairs.

2 Pass the left-hand pair over the centre pair, and move the centre pair to the left. What was the left-hand pair becomes the centre pair.

3 Pass the right-hand pair over the centre pair and move the centre pair to the right. What was the right-hand pair becomes the centre pair.

4 Repeat the previous two steps until the required length of plait has been worked.

5 When the glue has dried, trim the edges of the Aida with sharp scissors, fairly close to the framework, leaving just enough room for the plaited edging to be stuck on (about $^1/_8$in or 3.2mm). To add the trimming, start by pinning the knotted end of the plait to the back of the Aida, behind one of the front legs. Using dressmakers' pins to hold it in place, carefully stick the plait around the edge of the Aida with tacky glue, working across the bottom edge of the chair side, up and around the edge of the back, and along the bottom of the other side until you arrive back at the starting place. Leave enough plait to tuck behind the Aida and the leg, and tie the plait off neatly, then cut off the excess. Glue the ends firmly to the back of the Aida, hiding them as much as possible, and use a pin to hold them until the glue has set. Remove all the pins, and when finished, you should have a reasonable representation of a basketwork chair.

FINAL ARRANGEMENT

Arrange the tub, planters, pot plants, and sink garden to your satisfaction. When you are happy with your arrangement, the pots and planters can be held in place with a tiny bit of double-sided sticky tape or, if you want to be able to move your plants about, use small pieces of Blu-Tack, which shouldn't damage the surfaces too much when removed. Then place your chair in position ready for a member of the doll family to relax and admire the beautiful floral display.

CHAPTER 12

POND AND ROCKERY

It is, obviously, possible to simulate the stones of a rockery by using the real thing – only smaller. You could simply collect together a selection of suitably shaped stones, shingle, and pebbles, but this makes for a very heavy garden. If you want to use the real thing, then gather more than you think you will need, because when it comes down to it you will probably find that some stones are more suitable than others and you will discard many of them. An alternative is to cut chunks of Oasis and shape them to imitate rockery stones, then paint them. This is the method I have used.

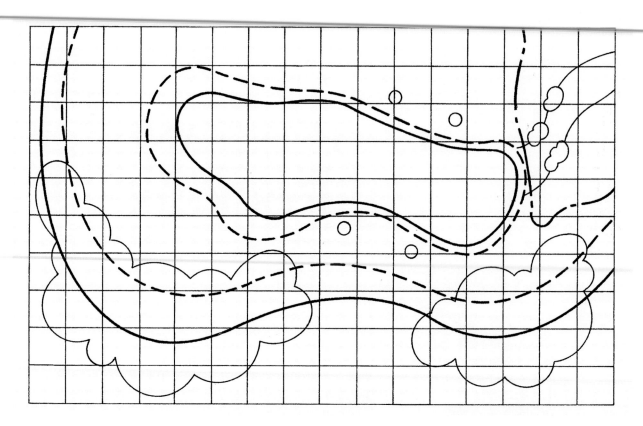

Ground plan for the Pond and Rockery garden. See text for explanation of the 'contour' lines.

MATERIALS

❋ Baseboard: 9mm (³/₈in) MDF, 16 x 10in (406 x 254mm)
❋ Plasterboard, 16 x 9in (406 x 229mm) and 10 x 8in (254 x 203mm)
❋ Railway layout grass mat
❋ Clear nail polish
❋ Clear styrene sheet, or similar, about ¹/₃₂ or ¹/₃₆in (0.8 or 1.6mm) thick
❋ PVA glue
❋ Silicone sealant, clear
❋ Tacky glue
❋ Railway layout foam flock material, yellow and red
❋ Dried grasses and flowers
❋ Aquarium greenery
❋ Coloured paper
❋ Clear UHU
❋ Orange Fimo or gold paper
❋ Twigs, or kebab skewers
❋ Reindeer moss
❋ Stones, or Oasis dried-flower arranging material
❋ Fix and Grout (or similar) tile cement

POND AND STREAM

To give depth to the pond I chose to use layers of plasterboard, left over from a ceiling. It is easy to cut with a craft knife if you score through the card surface on both sides and press the piece out. If it doesn't come out exactly as you wanted, don't worry – irregular edges can look very realistic. You may well find that your local builder has offcuts of plasterboard he will be glad to get rid of, but which will be big enough for your purpose.

1 Cut one piece of plasterboard to the smaller size and one to the larger size given in the materials list. Enlarge the plans and transfer them to the relevant pieces of plasterboard as explained on pages 24–6. On the larger piece, mark the shape shown by the thick, solid line on the ground plan; the dotted line on the plan is the shape for the smaller piece. Mark a cross on one corner of each enlargement and on the same corner of both sides of the plasterboard, so that the plans can be accurately transferred to *both* sides of the plasterboard. When marking the underside of the plasterboard, remember to turn the tracing paper over so that the side you have drawn on is next to the plasterboard; and check that the two corner crosses coincide.

2 Cut the pond shapes out by cutting through the surface card of the plasterboard on the lines marked on both sides. A push or sharp tap should remove the centre piece for the pond. It will probably not come out with even edges, but worry not, this will be dealt with next.

3 Put the two pieces of plasterboard together, the smaller one on top, so that the holes are over one another and the back edges of the plasterboard are flush with each other. Use a strong, sharp knife, such as a Stanley knife, to trim around the hole so that there is a slope from the top of the small piece to the bottom of the large piece: this will form the banks of the pond, so it doesn't have to be the same angle all round, or too smooth and even. Trim the other irregular edge, which will be the rockery bank. Before separating the two pieces of plasterboard write TOP on the small piece – it won't show when you've finished.

4 Lay the smaller piece of plasterboard on clear styrene sheet, with TOP upwards, and draw around the bottom of the pond shape onto the clear sheet. If you have difficulty in drawing on the plastic sheet, use one of the special pens for writing on film. Cut the sheet about $1/2$in (12.7mm) larger all the way round the shape marked. This will be the pond water surface.

5 Glue the larger piece of plasterboard onto the baseboard with PVA glue, in the position shown. Cut the piece shown by the chain-dotted (dashed and dotted) line on the ground plan from a spare bit of plasterboard, mark the stream onto this from the plan, and carefully cut through the top surface of the plasterboard to remove plaster to about half the thickness of the board. Glue this piece to the right-hand side of the smaller piece of plasterboard as shown on the plan.

The pond with its goldfish and water lilies.

6   Paint the baseboard inside the pond area, including the edges of the plasterboard, with blue/grey/green acrylic paint. On the smaller piece of plasterboard, paint the edges inside the pond shape and the stream area with a sandy colour. To test the effect, lay the piece of plastic sheet and then the small piece of plasterboard over the top temporarily, and if you are not satisfied, remove them again and repaint the areas until you are satisfied.

7   To simulate plants within the pond, stick small pieces of ferny artificial fish tank weed onto the base inside the pond area. Small areas of green foam railway scatter material stuck to tacky glue can also be added. When you are happy with this, carefully blow out any unwanted bits. Make tiny fishes from orange Fimo or gold paper, no more than $1/2$in (12.7mm) long, and stick them to the bits of pond weed with clear UHU glue.

8   Lay the clear plastic shape over the pond base and glue it to the top of the plasterboard with clear glue; then glue the second piece of plasterboard over the top with PVA glue.

GRASS AREA

Cut a piece of grass mat railway layout material about 22 x 15in (559 x 381mm). Temporarily cover the whole of the garden with this, leaving an equal overlap all round. By pressing gently with your fingers you should be able to feel the edge of the pond area. Mark the approximate shape of the pond onto the surface of the grass material. Remove the grass material and cut out the pond area marked, then replace over the pond to check the fit and trim again if necessary. Mark and cut out the grass material from the stream area in a similar way. Remove the grass mat again and apply PVA glue to a strip about 1in (25mm) wide around the pond and stream areas. Carefully press the grass material in place around the edge of the pond and stream. Lift the edges of the grass and apply PVA glue to the remaining plasterboard area, a bit at a time; gently mould and shape the grass over the remaining area, before pressing it firmly in place. Stick the excess grass material to the edges and underside of the baseboard, trimming as necessary.

ROCKERY

Now you can arrange the stones for the rockery; this will probably take three or four goes before you are satisfied. Carefully remove bits of grass mat from beneath one stone at a time and fix the stones in place with tile cement. When the cement is dry, paint it a dirty earth colour with acrylic paints.

A piece of clingfilm over the grass around the stones avoids getting the grass irreparably covered with bits of tile cement.

POND PLANTS

By making small holes in the plastic sheet with a darning needle or awl, you can push the stems of the plants through to the bed of the pond.

FLAG IRIS

The ones shown were made from crepe paper as described on page 52, but they could be made from fabric or recycled silk flowers. I suggest leaves of grass-like plastic aquarium weed.

BULRUSH OR REED MACE

Wrap a small bit of synthetic cotton wool tightly around the top of a piece of covered wire, preferably brown, to about ³/₄in (19.1mm) down the wire. Apply PVA glue to the cotton wool, and squeeze lightly into shape. When the glue has dried, use acrylic paint or wood stain to colour the cotton wool brown. Make two or three of these. The leaves shown in the photograph consist of long bristles from a cheap brown-bristled sweeping brush. Make a small hole in the top of the plastic pond surface and push the wire stems down through this to the pond base, then push some brush bristles into the same hole and secure them all in place with clear glue around the hole.

Pond plants include bulrushes and flag irises.

REEDS

Use grass-like aquarium leaves, and dried grass heads with their stems shortened to suit, or bunches of brush bristles, as used for the bulrush, to simulate clumps of reeds. Plant them in the pond as for the bulrush.

OTHER POND PLANTS

Plastic aquarium plants of various kinds were used to form the other pond plants, in some cases much cut down and reassembled.

WATER LILIES

Water-lily leaf pattern.

Some kinds of plastic aquarium plant leaves are very suitable for water-lily leaves. They need to be fairly round and flat, and about ¹/₂in (12.7 mm) to ³/₄in (19.1mm) in diameter. If the leaves are a bit too large, or you would prefer to make fabric leaves, a cutting pattern is given opposite. The water-lily flowers can be simulated by using small plastic or fabric flowers, or by making paper ones from tissue paper as for a camellia (see page 41), but using larger circles of paper. Glue the leaves to the top of the pond surface with clear glue, and then glue the flowers to the leaves.

POND SURFACE

The holes made to insert pond plants can be sealed using clear silicone sealant, either the DIY version or the one intended for sealing aquariums, which can be smoothed with a wet finger if you work quickly. Tiny ripples can be created on the pond surface with clear UHU or nail varnish, depending on the type of clear sheet used (try it first on a scrap bit in case the glue acts as a solvent for that particular plastic and you melt a hole!), or the same type of clear silicone sealant mentioned above. It looks most convincing if you create ripples spreading out in circles from the base of each plant.

STREAM

Glue a few bits of gravel or very small stones onto the stream bed, and one or two bits of green foam. Use clear silicone sealant, as above, to create the water in the stream. Apply an even layer over the stream bed and down to the pond surface. Smooth the surface with a well-moistened finger. You will have to work quite quickly or the surface will set before you get it smooth. An alternative is to apply a number of coats of Humbrol Clear Fix, clear nail varnish, or clear glue, allowing each layer to dry thoroughly before applying the next.

Add a few bits of aquarium greenery and coloured reindeer moss to the sides of the stream for plants and flowers.

RUSTIC BRIDGE

The bridge looks most effective if you use fairly straight, well-dried twigs about ³/₁₆in (4.8mm) to ¹/₄in (6.4mm) diameter, but kebab skewers about ³/₁₆in diameter could be used instead, and would look best if they were stained. The boards on the walkway are made from ³/₃₂in (2.4mm) thick balsa wood.

CUTTING LIST

✿ Main posts	3¼in	(82.6mm)	cut 4
✿ Lower rails	3½in	(88.9mm)	cut 2
✿ Handrails	5in	(127mm)	cut 2
✿ Walkway supports	4⅜in	(111.1mm)	cut 2
✿ Centre uprights	2¼in	(57.2mm)	cut 2
✿ Diagonals	2¾in	(69.9mm) approximately	cut 4
✿ Boards	2¼in	(57.2mm)	cut 16

The rustic bridge.

Only approximate measurements can be given for the diagonals, as the exact length will depend on the material you use, so they will have to be cut 'to fit'.

1 Cut the main posts, handrails, and lower rails to the lengths given in the cutting list. Then shape one end of each main post to accept the handrail as shown, and both ends of the lower rails to fit snugly between the main posts. Both ends of the centre uprights will also need shaping similarly. If you intend to stain your bridge, then stain the pieces as they are cut and shaped, before you start gluing.

2 Assemble and glue together two main posts, one handrail, one lower rail, and one centre rail to form the framework for the first side. Make sure that the handrail is set on top of the main posts so that the overhang is equal at each end, that all corners are right angles, and that the centre upright is in the centre. Cut two diagonals to fit, stain them if necessary, and then glue in place. Make the second side in the same way.

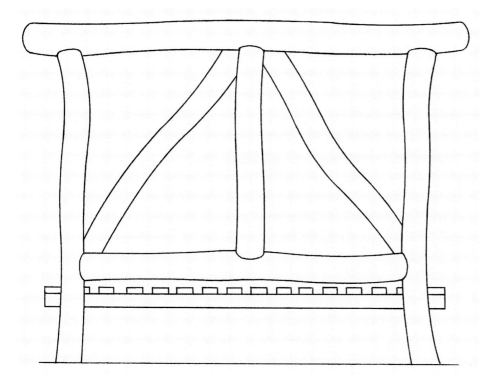

Full-size plan for the rustic bridge (see overleaf for plan of walkway).

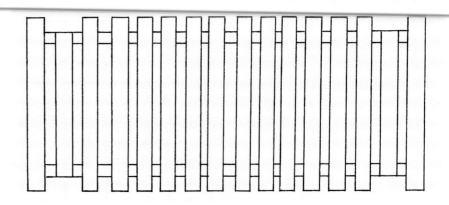

Full-size plan for the bridge walkway.

3   Cut the two walkway supports as given in the cutting list. Lay one support in position on one of the bridge sides and mark where the main post comes; shape these areas to fit snugly onto the main posts. Stain if necessary and glue firmly in position. Repeat this for the second walkway support and the second bridge side.

Cut the boards from ³/₃₂in (2.4mm) thick balsa wood. They are cut to various widths from about ³/₁₆in (4.8mm) to ⁵/₁₆in (7.9mm), and stained if necessary.

4   The two sides of the bridge can now be joined together with the walkway boards. Set the bridge sides upright, with their ends in line and the walkway supports on the inside. Start by gluing one board to the tops of the walkway supports at each end of the bridge, overlapping each side by about ¹/₈in (3.2mm), and check that the bridge is square. You will need to trim the boards which go between the main posts to length, as they will be shorter than the others, before gluing them in place. Glue the rest of the boards across the bridge, spacing them reasonably evenly.

PLANTING

I chose to keep this fairly simple, as creating the pond is complicated enough! Dried plant material was used for the two greyish bushes. Feathery reddish-coloured plastic aquarium weed was chopped down to form the clump to the back of the pond. Similar green aquarium weed was used as a basis for a yellow-flowered plant, the flowers being formed from yellow stamens and florets (see page 36), stuck to covered wire with tacky glue. The rest of the bushes are just chopped-up aquarium plants, as are the various green plants around the edge of the pond and stream. To plant the bushes, bore a hole through the grass mat and into the plasterboard with an awl or something similar. Then the plants can be stuck in with PVA glue.

PLANTING THE ROCKERY

Most of the plants I used on the rockery were created on a basis of reindeer moss. Nicely mounded pieces of green reindeer moss were turned into pansy plants (see page 53). Other green reindeer moss clumps were coated with tacky glue and pressed into foam railway layout material, some yellow and some red, or had stamen flowers added (see pages 29 and 30). A few pieces of pink dried flower material were pushed into some gaps, and pieces of dried bright blue statice were stuck in between other rocks.

The remaining gaps between stones were filled with reindeer moss of various colours. The ferns are made from yet another aquarium plant, which actually had large fern-like leaves. The ferns I created were made from individual bracts of the larger fern bunched together and stuck into a hole between the rocks.

This is a relatively quick and easy way of planting the rockery, but any number of variations is possible using dried flowers, or handmade flowers such as begonias (see page 40), petunias (see page 51), or other plants of any kind you choose.

Finally, set the bridge in position over the pond, as shown in the photograph. You can, of course, fix the bridge permanently by gluing it down, but I didn't glue mine, so that I can move it to dust the pond surface.

The left-hand rockery.

The right-hand rockery.

CHAPTER 13

COTTAGE GARDEN

Here you can create the olde worlde charm of a cottage garden, with its white fencing, covered well, rustic seat, and herbaceous borders. For planting the garden shown here I have chosen to use mainly handmade flowers with aquarium plant mat greenery, reindeer moss, and artificial stamens, dried plant material being used only for the tree.

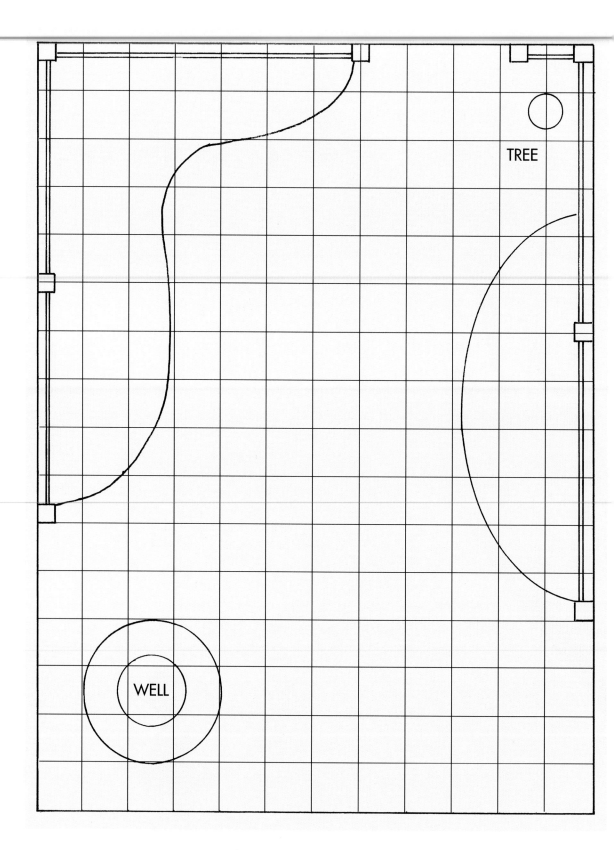

Ground plan for the Cottage Garden.

- ❀ Baseboard: 9mm ($^3/_8$in) MDF or similar, 16 x 12in (406 x 305mm)
- ❀ Well: Oasis round block; balsa wood $^1/_4$in (6.4mm) square, $^1/_4$ x $^3/_{32}$in (6.4 x 2.4mm) strip, and $^1/_2$in (12.7mm) diameter dowel; thin card; $^1/_{32}$in (0.8mm) model-making plywood
- ❀ Fence and gate: flat wooden lollipop sticks, wood $^3/_8$in (9.5mm) square and $^1/_4$ x $^1/_8$in (6.4 x 3.2mm) strip, florists' wire, empty drinks can, fast-setting wood adhesive, UHU or superglue
- ❀ Rustic chair: twigs or kebab skewers
- ❀ Railway layout grass mat
- ❀ PVA glue
- ❀ Handmade flowers and plants as detailed
- ❀ Aquarium greenery
- ❀ Rectangular Oasis brick
- ❀ Reindeer moss

BASEBOARD

Enlarge the plan and transfer to the MDF baseboard.

FLOWERBEDS

I used Oasis block material for the flowerbeds. Cut the block into slabs about $^5/_8$in (15.9mm) thick, as for the walls for the Walled Garden project (see page 77). Mark the shapes for the flowerbeds onto the slabs from the enlarged plan. Cut the shapes out carefully with a craft knife, cutting just outside the lines marked so that you have a bit extra to trim if necessary to fit neatly to the grass edge.

GRASS

I chose to extend the grass mat to cover the baseboard edges. If you want to do this you will need an extra 1in (25mm) all round the outside edges, so take this into account when marking the grass mat plan onto the material. Transfer the enlarged plan to the back of the material (see pages 24–6). Cut it out carefully and check the fit on the baseboard.

ASSEMBLY

1   The flowerbeds and grass mat can now be fitted to the baseboard. It is best to have a dry run to make sure everything goes together properly before being stuck down. The Oasis flowerbed blocks can be shaped so that there is a bit of a slope on the edges where they meet the grass. Position them on the baseboard and lay the grass mat in position over the baseboard and the Oasis to check that they fit neatly. Make any necessary adjustments to either or both. Remove the grass material carefully so that the Oasis is not disturbed and then mark around the flowerbeds to give the actual positions that they will occupy. Take off the Oasis, apply PVA glue to the area marked on the baseboard, and glue the flowerbeds in place.

2   The grass mat can now partially be stuck in position. Apply the glue to the top area of the baseboard but not to the edges. Carefully position the grass and press firmly to the baseboard. Leave the edges overhanging evenly.

3   Now the edges can be stuck down, but be careful whilst tidying up the edges that you don't damage the Oasis flowerbeds. Apply PVA glue to one edge of the baseboard at a time, turn the grass mat over the edge, and press firmly in position. Work round the baseboard, sticking down the grass to each edge. Ignore the excess at each corner for now, but squeeze the corners together as tightly as possible. When the glue has dried, cut the grass material at each corner vertically and level with the corner. Turn the grass under the baseboard, overlapping at the corners. Mitre the corners underneath by cutting through both layers diagonally from the outside edge towards the centre of the board, and remove the loose bits of grass. Use PVA glue to stick the grass mat to the bottom of the baseboard.

FENCE AND GATE

1   Cut 43 lollipop sticks to 2$\frac{1}{2}$in (63.5mm) long for palings, making sure that their lower ends are cut squarely. Cut the remaining parts according to the cutting list.

CUTTING LIST

❀ Fence rails –	$\frac{1}{4}$ x $\frac{1}{8}$in	(6.4 x 3.2mm) strip:	
Left-hand side	4$\frac{3}{8}$in	(111.1mm)	cut 4
Right-hand side	5$\frac{1}{2}$in	(139.7mm)	cut 4
Rear	6$\frac{1}{2}$in	(165.1mm)	cut 2
	1in	(25mm)	cut 2

❀ Gate rails – $1/4$ x $1/8$in (6.4 x 3.2mm) strip:
        3in   (76mm)   cut 2
        $3^1/2$in (88.9mm)   cut 1
❀ Fence posts – $3/8$ x $3/8$in (9.5 x 9.5mm):
        $3^1/4$in (82.6mm)   cut 8

The tree is made from dried grasses.

2 The fence panels are made by gluing lollipop sticks to the fence rails. Each panel consists of a top and a bottom rail with varying numbers of lollipop-stick palings equally spaced along them, and there is an equal gap at each end of the railings where they fit against the fence post. The gaps are, very approximately, $5/16$in (7.9mm).

I find it very helpful to use double-sided tape to keep the palings in place until the fence rails are glued on. Cut a piece about ½in (12.7mm) wide and 7in (178mm) long, stick this onto a spare piece of board, or the project baseboard, and assemble the fence panels on this.

PALINGS

❁ 2 left side panels   6 palings
❁ 2 right side panels   8 palings
❁ 1 rear panel   9 palings
❁ 1 rear panel   1 paling

4   To make a panel, lay one of the rails on the board alongside the tape and mark the board where each end of the rail comes. Take the correct number of lollipop sticks, as listed above, for the panel you are making and lay them lightly across the tape, repositioning them until the spacings are even. Remember to leave spaces between the first and last palings and the end of the rail where the posts will come. Make sure that the bottom edges of the palings are all level; I use a spare piece of square wood to do this. Use a piece about 14in (356mm) long and stick it temporarily to the assembly board with double-sided tape about 1in (25mm) below the tape you have already stuck on.

     When you have positioned the palings to your satisfaction they can be pressed onto the tape a little more. Don't press too hard or you will have difficulty in getting them off again – just enough so that they will stay where you put them.

A piece of clingfilm on the assembly board will prevent the fence from sticking to it during assembly.

5   The fence rails can now be glued on using a glue such as Evo-Stik extra-fast-setting wood adhesive. The ends of the rails should be level with each other, square with the lollipop-stick palings, and about ½in (12.7mm) from the top and bottom of them. Leave in place until the glue has set, then remove the whole panel very carefully from the tape and repeat until all the panels have been made.

6   To assemble the right-hand fence you need three fence posts and the two right-hand side panels. Lay these on the board so that the bottoms of the fence posts are against the square wood strip stuck to the assembly board. The fence panels are fitted between the posts, so lay these, palings downwards, between the posts to give the spacing. The bottoms of the panels need to be about ¼in (6.4mm) up from the bottoms of the posts. Apply wood glue to the ends of the rails of the panel, and press firmly onto the fence posts. Then do the same with the second panel. Check that all is square, evenly lined up, and the joints pressed firmly together; then leave to set. Assemble the left-hand side similarly.

7   Use a box, old books, or whatever comes to hand to support the finished left-hand side fence so that the rear corner post lies flat on the board with its foot against the square piece of wood, and the rest of the fence sticks up vertically. The palings should be on the outside, i.e. next to the support. The large rear fence panel can now be positioned, with the paling side downward,

between the corner post of the left-hand fence and another post placed to the right of it. Glue in place as before and leave until the glue sets hard.

The other side fence and the small rear fence section can now be assembled and glued together similarly. Remember that the support will need to be on the opposite side so that the palings of the side fence are next to it and the rear fence panel will be fixed to the left of the corner post.

You should now have two L-shaped sections of completed fencing with the palings all on the outside. These can now be painted with white acrylic or enamel paint and left to dry. I used matt paint, as cottage railings were often limewashed.

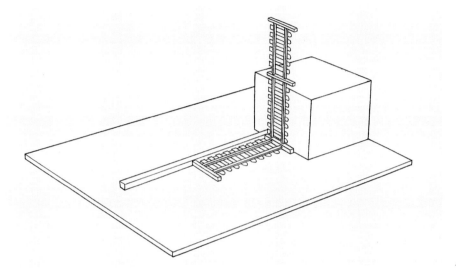

Assembling the garden fence.

8 The gate is made in a similar way to the fence panels, with five palings glued to the two railings, but this time the first and last palings must be flush with the end of the railings.

The gate, with its working hinges and latch.

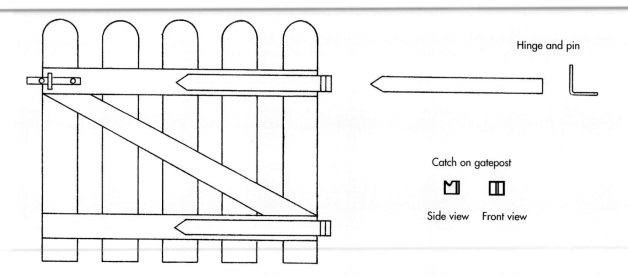

Hinge and pin

Catch on gatepost

Side view   Front view

Full-size pattern for gate.

When the glue is set and with the gate flat on the board, palings downwards, lay the cross brace diagonally across the gate and mark the ends which need to be trimmed to fit between the top and bottom rails. This should mean cutting the cross brace at approximately 45° at each end.

Cut hinges from thin plastic sheet or thin metal from a drinks can, or something of similar thickness. The metal can be cut with an old pair of scissors. Wrap one end of each strip round a piece of thick, stiff florists' wire to form a loop, and glue together with clear UHU all-purpose glue for the plastic or superglue for the metal, keeping your fingers well clear. Paint them matt black, and when dry glue in position on the gate crossbars. A gate catch is also shown on the drawing in case you wish to include this. Simply follow the drawing, paint matt black, and glue in position on the gate and fence post.

9 Stand the fence sections in position on the grass, making sure there is enough room for the gate and hinges by hanging the gate temporarily. Cut two pieces of the stiff florists' wire about ³⁄₄in (19.1mm) long and bend them in the middle at a right angle for gate hangers. Hold the gate in position and mark the positions of the hinges on the fence post. Make holes in the post just below the bottom of each hinge position. Apply glue to one end of each gate hanger and push them into the holes so that they point vertically upwards and there is just room for the ends of the hinges. Hang the gate by slipping the two hinges over the hangers. Make sure that the gate can be closed properly.

10 Mark around the fence posts on the grass with a pencil, then remove the gate and fence sections. Make diagonal cuts from corner to corner across the squares marked on the grass. Carefully loosen the grass mat from the baseboard to lift the edges, and fold back to leave a square of the baseboard exposed to allow the fence to be glued to the baseboard; but do not glue it until after the tree has been installed (see below).

11 Once the tree is in position, use wood glue on the bottom of the posts to glue the fence in place, checking that the gate still works. When the posts are firmly fixed and the glue has dried, use a sharp craft knife to trim the grass around them.

TREE

1 I used dried grasses for my tree, but a somewhat different tree could be made in a similar way with dried sea lavender, sprayed green. Bunch the dried grasses together and bind tightly with cotton, securing with tacky glue.

2 To create a trunk for the tree I used air-drying clay, with which I covered the grass stems and formed a root base spreading out all around about 1in (25mm) from the trunk in an irregular manner. When dry, the clay was painted with a fairly light brown acrylic paint and streaked with a darker brownish-green colour.

3 Stand the tree in position on the grass mat and mark round the roots. Use a craft knife to cut through the grass mat in the place marked for the tree, and scrape off the grass within this area. Then stick the tree firmly to the baseboard with PVA glue. The fence and gate can now be fixed to the baseboard (see above).

WELL

A traditional covered well.

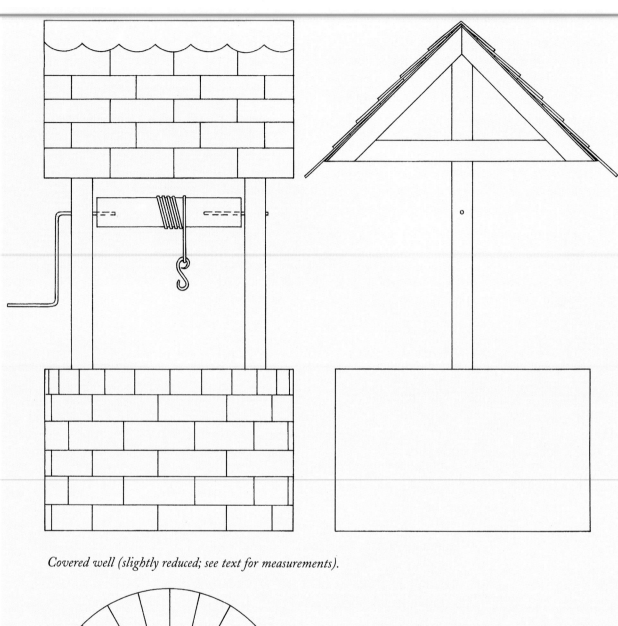

Covered well (slightly reduced; see text for measurements).

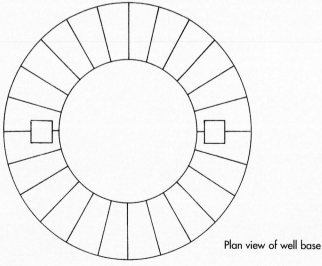

Plan view of well base

1 Make the base from a round Oasis block approximately 3in (76mm) diameter and 2in (51mm) high. On one end of the block, mark the smaller circle shown in the plan view of the well base, and use a narrow-bladed knife to make a vertical cut into the end of the block along this line. Carefully scoop out the central area within this cut, keeping the sides as near vertical as possible. Use an awl or similar pointed tool to mark a brick top edging to the well and courses of brickwork around the sides. Paint the brickwork with varied reddish-brown shades of acrylic paint and allow to dry. Give it a weathered look by painting random bits with a much watered-down dark greenish-brown paint and dabbing with a tissue.

2 Cut the pieces for the roof support frame from $^1/_4$ x $^1/_4$in (6.4 x 6.4mm) and $^1/_4$ x $^3/_{32}$in (6.4 x 2.4mm) balsa wood to the patterns given and make holes in the two uprights to take the wire support and handle for the roller. Stain the wood a fairly dark brown; I used Colron walnut stain.

When the stain is dry the framework can be glued together as shown in the plan. Mark the top of the well wall for the position of the roof frame supports and make holes about $^3/_8$in (9.5mm) deep. Put some wood glue into the holes and insert the roof supports, making sure the uprights are vertical. Then leave to dry.

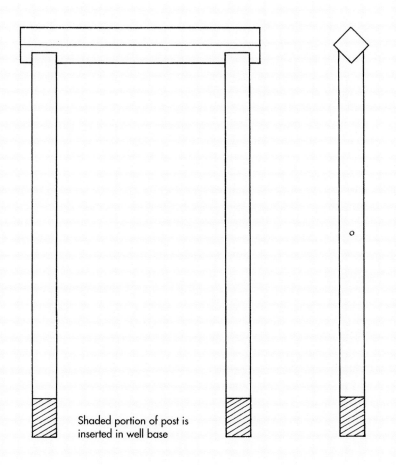

Shaded portion of post is inserted in well base

Full-size pattern for the well roof framework.

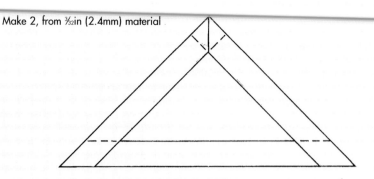

Make 2, from ³⁄₃₂in (2.4mm) material

Full-size pattern for the well gable.

3 A 1³⁄₄in (44.5mm) long piece of ⁵⁄₁₆in (7.9mm) diameter balsa dowel was used for the roller in the model shown, but any similar-sized material will do. Stain this the same colour as the frame. Make a handle and support pin for the roller from stiff florists' wire. For the support pin a straight piece 1in (25mm) long is needed, or alternatively a straight dressmaker's pin about the same length. The handle needs a piece of wire 2¹⁄₂in (63.5mm) long, bent to the pattern given in the side elevation.

Fix the roller to the support frame by holding it in position between the uprights so that the centre of each end is in line with the holes in the uprights. Push the straight support pin through the hole in one of the uprights and into the end of the roller; then push the longer end of the handle through the hole into the other end of the roller.

Paint the handle matt black. Use brown button thread for a rope: glue one end of it to the centre of the roller and wind a few turns of thread around the roller to cover this end, then cut the thread to leave an end about 3in (76mm) long. Bend a small piece of wire to form an S-shaped hook, tie this to the end of the piece of thread, and trim to leave a loose end of only about ¹⁄₄in (6.4mm). A dab of tacky glue will tidy this up and stick it to the main thread.

4 The roof of the well is made from card, and tiled with thin wood shingles. Cut a piece of card 3in (76mm) wide and 5in (127mm) long. Fold this in half across the width to mark the centre for the ridge. I stained the card with the same stain as I used for the framework.

Apply tacky glue to the top surfaces of the roof support, position the card centrally, and press firmly onto the glue. Spring clothes pegs can be used to hold it tight to the framework until the glue sets. For the shingles I used ¹⁄₃₂in (0.8mm) model-making ply, basically because I had some bits left from something else. Any similar thickness wood will do, or failing all else, thin card would serve the purpose. A piece of material about 12in (305mm) long and 3in (76mm) wide will be needed. Cut long strips ³⁄₄in (19.1mm) wide and then cut across these at ³⁄₄in (19.1mm) intervals, to give you square wood shingles. Starting from the lower edge of the roof, glue the shingles on, overlapping the rows and cutting shingles in half as necessary, to the pattern shown.

Stain the shingles unevenly for a weathered look, and complete the roof by cutting a ridge trim from very thin card to the pattern given in the drawing. Paint this a dirty grey colour like old lead, and when dry stick in place across the top of the roof.

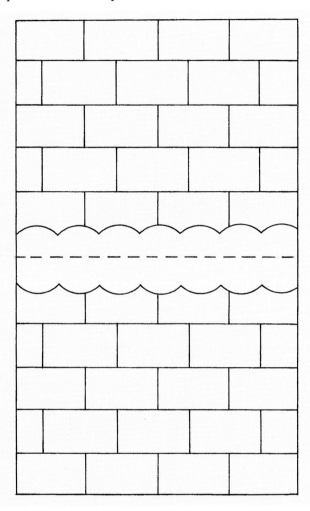

Full-size pattern for the well roof.

5 Cut a piece of thin card to the pattern given in the drawing as a basis for the wooden pail. Thin balsa is used for the wooden sides, with slats cut as shown. These are stained and then stuck to the card. I used a flat button 1in (25mm) in diameter for the base, and filled up the buttonholes. If the diameter of the base is not right the card and wood surround will not fit properly, so you could use a circle of balsa, as given on the drawing. Assemble the pail in the same way as the wooden tub in the Patio Garden project (see page 93). Cut $^1/_8$in (3.2mm) wide strips of black paper or very thin card painted black, and stick these around the pail for iron bands, as for the patio tub. A piece of florists' iron wire 2$^1/_2$in (63.5mm) long was used for the handle on the pail illustrated. Bend the wire at right angles about $^1/_4$in (6.4mm) from each end, and push these ends through the holes in the sides of the pail. Carefully squeeze the ends up towards the pail to form a hook and keep the handle on the pail.

The well's coopered bucket.

125

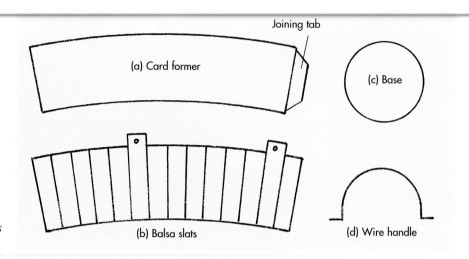

(a) Card former

Joining tab

(c) Base

(b) Balsa slats

(d) Wire handle

*Full-size patterns
for well bucket.*

FLOWERS AND PLANTS

Decide on your planting plan and make flowers and plants ready for planting. The plants and flowers I used for the garden shown in the photograph were mostly handmade as listed below.

Single-flowered hollyhocks (see pages 43–4) were made using red, yellow, and pink tissue paper with aquarium greenery for leaves.

The same method as detailed for hollyhocks was used to make a mallow plant with mauve/pink tissue, using smaller circles of paper than for the

*The left-hand border with its
colourful delphiniums, geraniums,
and carnations; the hollyhocks in
the rear border can also be seen.*

The mallow plant in the right-hand border.

Delphiniums dominate the right-hand border.

hollyhocks and shorter flower stems. The leaves are aquarium plastic plant mat with pointed oval leaves.

I made delphiniums (see pages 48–9) using table napkins to give me the shade of blue I wanted, and used aquarium plants for leaves.

A few larkspur (see page 49) in pink and white with aquarium leaves were used for medium-height plants.

Geranium flowers (see pages 46–7) were made using pink, dark red, white, and mauve tissue paper. I cheated on the leaves by again using plastic aquarium plants, doctoring the leaves to a round shape and to a suitable size, and adding the zonal markings with acrylic paint.

Double begonias (see page 40) made with deep yellow, orange, and dark red tissue are placed in fairly prominent positions. The same aquarium mat as for the mallow plant was used for the leaves. This was cut up to give short pieces which were bound together with fine wire, and the flowers were stuck into the Oasis between the leaves.

Carnations, made following the general instructions on page 56, were made with stranded embroidery thread in colours ranging from very dark to very pale pink, with Christmas-tree greenery for leaves.

Two large dahlia plants (see page 55), using fine crochet cotton in shaded pink and yellow with aquarium plant mat leaves, occupy opposite flowerbeds.

For the daisy flowers (see page 58) I used fine crochet cotton in pink and three shades of yellow, with feathery plastic aquarium greenery for the leaves.

The sprawling mat of colour at the edges of the beds is reindeer moss, just as it came, in pink, purple, and pale green. The tree roots are half hidden by small bits of reindeer moss glued to them, and the corner is made to look less bare by a small climber made from reindeer moss glued to covered wire.

For the base of the well, small clumps of low plants were made from reindeer moss with coloured artificial stamen flowers (see page 30), and stuck on in a random way.

Different kinds of fern were concocted from much larger aquarium plants cut into little bits and reassembled.

PLANTING

Start from the back of each flowerbed in turn with the tallest plants and push the bases of the plants firmly into the Oasis. Gradually work towards the front with shorter plants, finishing by sticking the clumps of reindeer moss to the Oasis to cover grass mat edges and simulate a border edging of aubrietia and similar plants.

RUSTIC CHAIR

1 Use well-dried twigs or wooden kebab sticks about $^3/_{16}$in (4.8mm) diameter.

The rustic chair. Note the simulated nail heads at the joints.

CUTTING LIST			
❀ Back legs	2$^7/_8$in	(73mm)	cut 2
❀ Front legs	2in	(51mm)	cut 2
❀ Arm rest	1$^3/_4$in	(44.5mm)	cut 2
❀ Back rails	1$^1/_2$in	(38.1mm)	cut 2
❀ Top back rail	2in	(25mm)	cut 1
❀ Back trims	1in	(25mm)	cut 3
❀ Side rails	1$^1/_2$in	(38.1mm)	cut 3
❀ Seat bars	1$^7/_8$in	(47.6mm)	cut 5

2 Assemble and glue the chair together in sections as shown. Use extra-fast-setting wood adhesive, or similar, to glue the chair together. First make the two side frames, then join these together with the back rails and seat bars. Cut the ends of the back trim pieces to fit, and glue them in place.

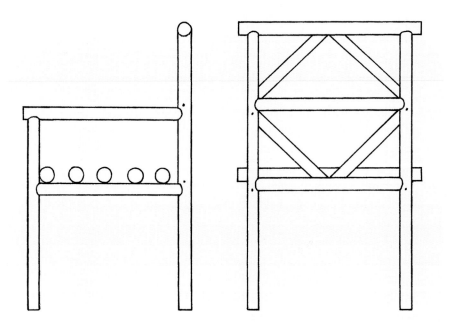

Full-size side and rear views of the rustic chair. The dots represent simulated nail heads.

3   I left my rustic chair natural and added pencil marks where the nail heads would be, but it could be stained, which should be done before the pieces are glued together so as to avoid light patches where the stain is blocked by glue. Alternatively, it could be painted with acrylics. Make sure that everything is dry before setting the chair in position to complete your cottage garden.

BUTTERFLY

Just for fun, I added a butterfly in my cottage garden. This was made from a small circle of orange tissue paper folded in half, with the edges trimmed for wing shapes. Then black markings were added to the opened-out shape and the butterfly fixed onto one of the leaves of a begonia plant.

A tiny butterfly, less than ¼in (6.4mm) across, on a begonia leaf.

A rear view of the Cottage Garden.

CHAPTER 14

GREENHOUSE GARDEN

I think of this greenhouse as 'Father's hideaway'. With all the pot plants, seedlings, tomato plants, etc. to be watered, he has plenty of excuses to 'escape' for a bit of peace and quiet. There is also plenty of space for the prize chrysanthemums to be carefully nurtured.

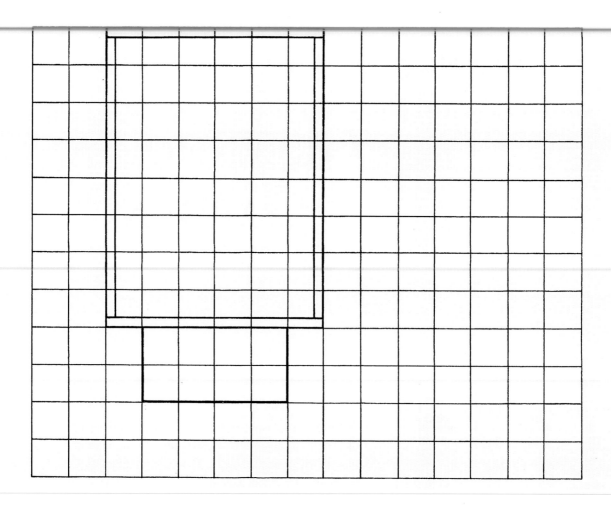

*Ground plan of
Greenhouse Garden.*

MATERIALS

- ❁ Baseboard: 9mm (³⁄₈in) MDF, 12 x 15in (305 x 381mm)
- ❁ Plastruct plastic sections as detailed on page 134
- ❁ Clear glazing sheet
- ❁ Railway layout ballast
- ❁ PVA glue
- ❁ All-purpose glue
- ❁ Plastic Weld (or similar) liquid cement
- ❁ Superglue
- ❁ Oasis blocks
- ❁ Balsa wood
- ❁ Aquarium greenery
- ❁ Bamboo skewers
- ❁ Fimo
- ❁ Magazine pictures
- ❁ Drinks can metal sheet or thin stiff card

- ❀ Electric wire
- ❀ Electricians' insulating tape
- ❀ Wheelbarrow wheel, or button
- ❀ Grass mat
- ❀ Very thick twig
- ❀ Bottle tops
- ❀ Das air-drying clay, terracotta
- ❀ Paint
- ❀ Tiny glass seed beads
- ❀ Crochet cotton: bright colours and white
- ❀ Embroidery thread
- ❀ Covered wire
- ❀ Thick plastic-coated garden wire

Instead of the usual wood strips I decided to try out some of the Plastruct small plastic section available from model shops, and by mail order from such firms as Hobby's. This looks a bit like the aluminium section used for the full-size greenhouses of today, particularly if it is coated with silvery paint. It made assembly of a greenhouse fairly easy, and the result is a firm structure. Glazing it with clear acrylic sheet is also easy as the two plastics stick together well. In keeping with the material, this greenhouse was designed as a contemporary one, and some contents of a similarly modern period are therefore included. Although not quite the right design, you can use this plan for an earlier period if you use the white Plastruct section, or give the plastic a coat of white paint before glazing, to imitate a whitened wooden greenhouse. Similarly it can be used for a cedar-type greenhouse if the plastic sections are given a coat of reddish-brown paint. The contents would have to be modified a bit to keep to a specific period.

BASEBOARD

Cut a baseboard to the sizes given above, and transfer an enlarged version of the plan to the baseboard as described on pages 24–6.

GREENHOUSE BASE

Cut 1/4in (6.4mm) square wooden strips to form a rectangle with outside dimensions of 8 x 6in (203 x 152mm) and fix firmly to the baseboard, as shown in the plan, with PVA glue. Paint the strips with brick-coloured masonry paint (Sandtex or similar) from a sample tin, and when dry, score lines through the paint for brickwork. 1/12-scale size for bricks would be about 3/4 x 1/4in (19.1 x 6.4mm).

PAVING, FLOWERBED, AND GRASS

In front of the greenhouse is a small area of rough paving stones; the surrounding area is mostly grass, apart from the area where the prize chrysanths are grown.

I recommend using a glass bottle with straight sides for rolling Das, and working on a piece of board covered with kitchen foil.

1   Make paving stones from Das air-drying clay. Roll the clay out to about $^1/_8$in (3.2mm) thick and cut through to form approximately 1in (25mm) squares. Either use terracotta-coloured clay for quarry-tile paving (in Norfolk, where I live, they are called *pamments*), or use grey Das and paint when dry with Sandtex. When dry, glue the paving in position with PVA glue.

2   Use Oasis or Dryfoam styrofoam for the flowerbed. Cut a slice about $^1/_2$in (12.7mm) thick, 4in (102mm) long, and 1in (25mm) wide. Glue to the baseboard with PVA glue, and when this is dry, shape the edges of the styrofoam to slope from the centre of the flowerbed to the outer edges.

3   Cut grass mat material to cover the remaining area, and glue in position as shown on the layout plan.

GREENHOUSE

The greenhouse itself can be made quite easily from the information given on the drawings. In view of the large number of small parts, it is easier to explain how it is made in drawings than in words.

The Plastruct sections used are as follows:

T-section: T-4, $^1/_8$ x $^1/_8$in (3.2 x 3.2mm)

Angle: A-4, $^1/_8$ x $^1/_8$in (3.2 x 3.2mm) and A-3, $^3/_{32}$ x $^3/_{32}$in (2.4 x 2.4mm)

H-section column: H-3, $^3/_{32}$ x $^3/_{32}$in (2.4 x 2.4mm)

Flat strip: cut to $^1/_4$in (6.4mm) and $^5/_{16}$in (7.9mm) wide

I-section beam: B-6, $^3/_{16}$ x $^3/_{32}$in (4.8 x 2.4mm) and B-8, $^1/_4$ x $^1/_8$in (6.4 x 3.2mm)

Channel: C-6, $^3/_{16}$ x $^1/_{16}$in (4.8 x 1.6mm)

1   Cut plastic pieces of the sections and sizes shown to the lengths given in the drawings. Using Plastic Weld or similar liquid cement, according to the manufacturer's instructions, assemble the framework section by section as shown.

2   Make two side assemblies, one rear end assembly, and one front end assembly with doorway to the plans given.

The unglazed framework of the greenhouse.

3   Using A-3 angle to reinforce the inside of each corner, stick the side and end sections together to form the main body of the greenhouse, then fix the roof ridge in place and add the roof side spars. Make a vent and a door to the plans as shown. Fix the vent in place in the roof frame; I fixed mine in an open position, but yours could be either open or closed.

4   At this stage I gave my greenhouse a coat of paint. Remove the door and spray this separately. Spray the greenhouse framework inside and out with a coat of Plasti-kote spray paint, remembering the safety rules on page 11. I used aluminium-coloured paint for my modern greenhouse, but you could use any of the alternatives suggested above.

5   Cut clear glazing sheet into panes of suitable size to fit the framework and glaze the greenhouse, then set safely to one side and make the inner components. The greenhouse shown here was left unglazed to avoid unwanted reflections in the photographs.

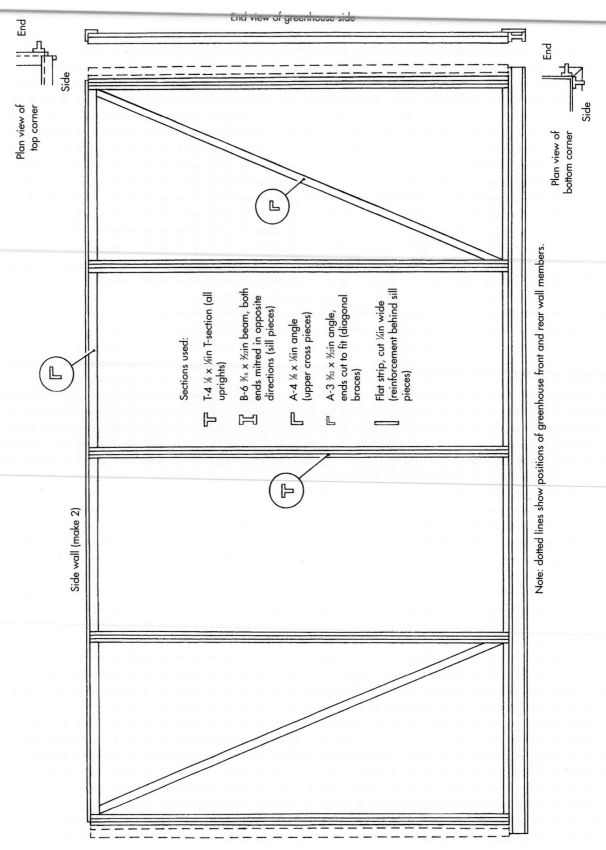

End view of greenhouse side

Plan view of top corner

End

Side

Plan view of bottom corner

End

Side

Sections used:

T-4 ⅛ x ⅛in T-section (all uprights)

B-6 ³⁄₁₆ x ³⁄₃₂in beam, both ends mitred in opposite directions (sill pieces)

A-4 ⅛ x ⅛in angle (upper cross pieces)

A-3 ³⁄₃₂ x ³⁄₃₂in angle, ends cut to fit (diagonal braces)

Flat strip, cut ¼in wide (reinforcement behind sill pieces)

Side wall (make 2)

Note: dotted lines show positions of greenhouse front and rear wall members.

Greenhouse side wall, drawn full size.

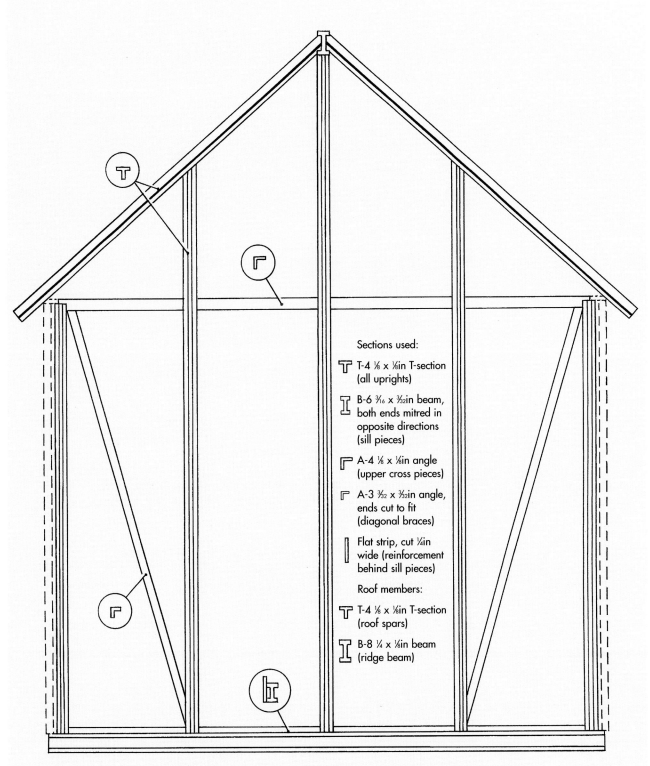

Sections used:

⊤ T-4 ⅛ x ⅛in T-section
(all uprights)

I B-6 ³⁄₁₆ x ³⁄₃₂in beam,
both ends mitred in
opposite directions
(sill pieces)

Γ A-4 ⅛ x ⅛in angle
(upper cross pieces)

Γ A-3 ³⁄₃₂ x ³⁄₃₂in angle,
ends cut to fit
(diagonal braces)

| Flat strip, cut ¼in
wide (reinforcement
behind sill pieces)

Roof members:

⊤ T-4 ⅛ x ⅛in T-section
(roof spars)

I B-8 ¼ x ⅛in beam
(ridge beam)

Note: dotted lines show positions of greenhouse side wall members. Since lower ends of roof spars rest on the side walls as shown, roof construction cannot begin until all four walls have been assembled.

Rear elevation of greenhouse, drawn full size.

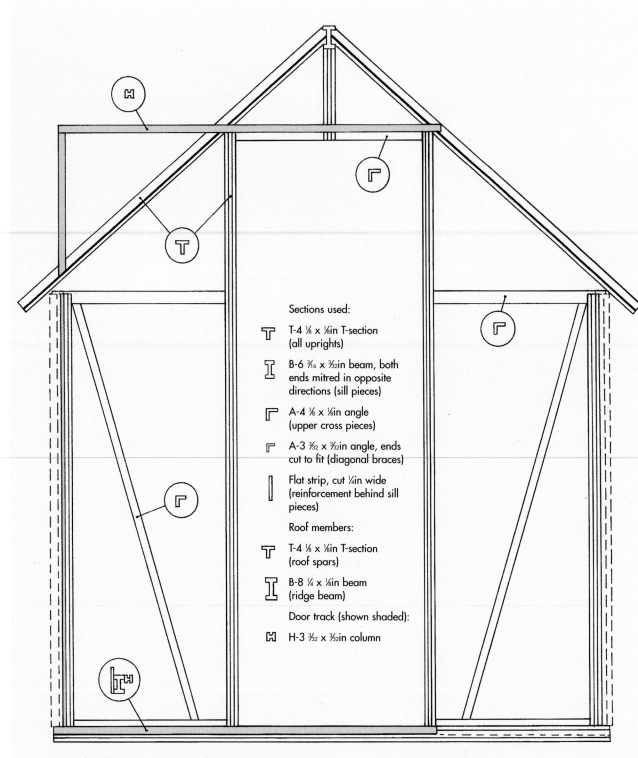

Sections used:

T   T-4 ⅛ x ⅛in T-section (all uprights)

I   B-6 ³⁄₁₆ x ³⁄₃₂in beam, both ends mitred in opposite directions (sill pieces)

Γ   A-4 ⅛ x ⅛in angle (upper cross pieces)

Γ   A-3 ³⁄₃₂ x ³⁄₃₂in angle, ends cut to fit (diagonal braces)

I   Flat strip, cut ¼in wide (reinforcement behind sill pieces)

Roof members:

T   T-4 ⅛ x ⅛in T-section (roof spars)

I   B-8 ¼ x ⅛in beam (ridge beam)

Door track (shown shaded):

H   H-3 ³⁄₃₂ x ³⁄₃₂in column

Note: dotted lines show positions of greenhouse side wall members. Since lower ends of roof spars rest on the side walls as shown, roof construction cannot begin until all four walls have been assembled.

Front elevation of greenhouse, drawn full size (door track shown shaded).

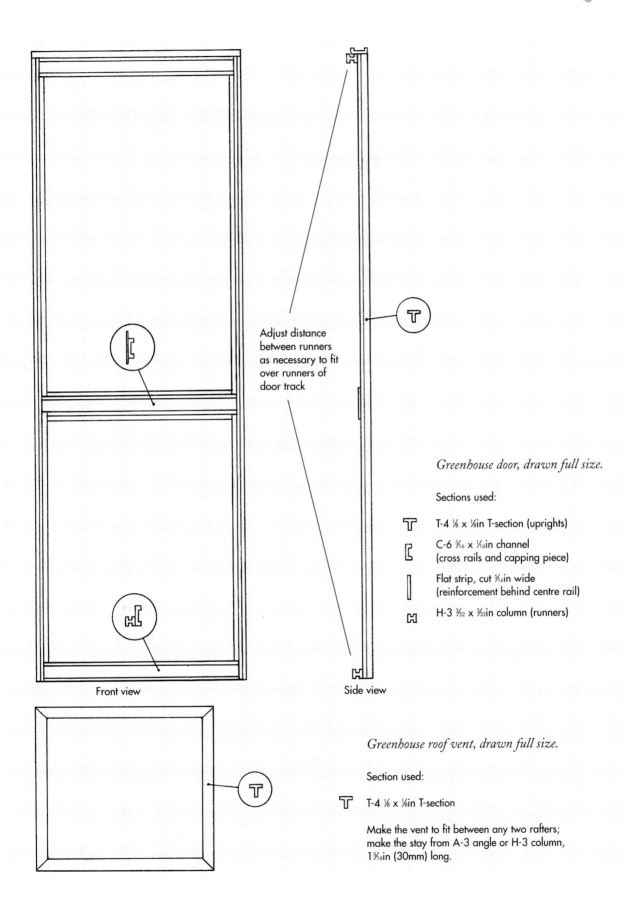

Adjust distance
between runners
as necessary to fit
over runners of
door track

Front view

Side view

Greenhouse door, drawn full size.

Sections used:

T-4 ⅛ x ⅛in T-section (uprights)

C-6 ³⁄₁₆ x ⅛in channel
(cross rails and capping piece)

Flat strip, cut ³⁄₁₆in wide
(reinforcement behind centre rail)

H-3 ³⁄₃₂ x ³⁄₃₂in column (runners)

Greenhouse roof vent, drawn full size.

Section used:

T-4 ⅛ x ⅛in T-section

Make the vent to fit between any two rafters;
make the stay from A-3 angle or H-3 column,
1³⁄₁₆in (30mm) long.

STAGING

The staging and seed boxes.

1 The staging inside the greenhouse can be left natural, stained to a colour of your choice, or even painted. If you intend to stain it, then do so before starting on the assembly, so that there will be no light-coloured patches where the glue has blocked the stain. Make the staging of balsa wood cut to the sections and lengths in the cutting list.

Cutting list

❀ $\frac{1}{4}$ x $\frac{1}{8}$in (6.4 x 3.2mm):	2$\frac{1}{2}$in	(63.5mm)	cut 6
	1$\frac{1}{4}$in	(31.8mm)	cut 7
❀ $\frac{1}{4}$ x $\frac{3}{32}$in (6.4 x 2.4mm):	6$\frac{1}{2}$in	(165.1mm)	cut 4
	5$\frac{7}{8}$in	(149.2mm)	cut 2
	2$\frac{7}{8}$in	(73mm)	cut 4

If your material for the uprights is not exactly to size, I suggest that you cut the four pieces for the lower planking a little longer than listed above, so that the planks can be cut 'to fit' during assembly.

2 Assemble two end frames and one centre frame, as shown in the front view and side views. Make sure that the uprights and cross battens are square with each other and glue together, clamping the joints firmly until the glue dries.

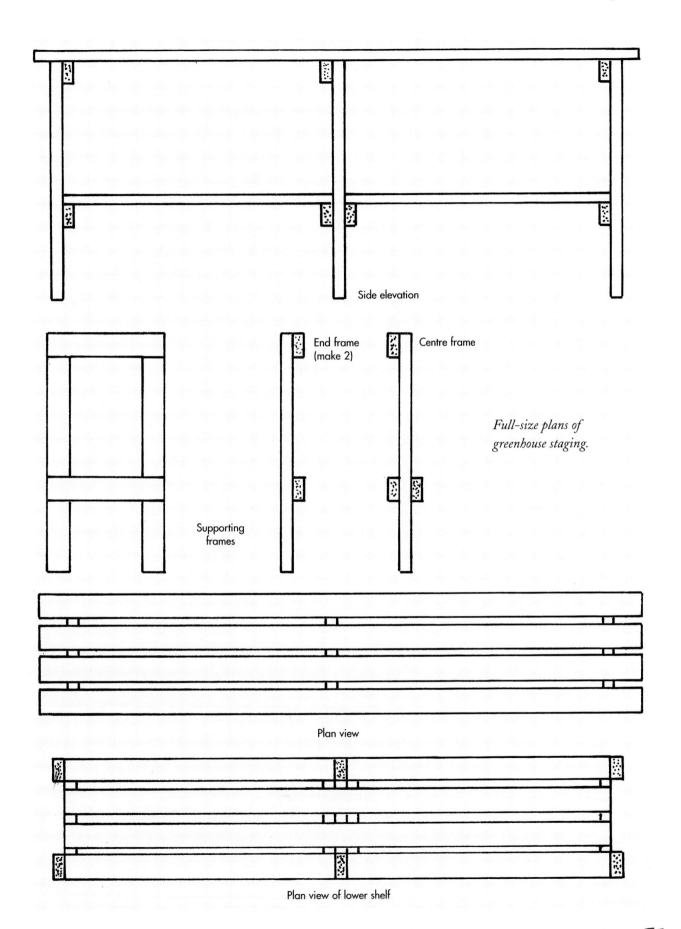

Side elevation

End frame
(make 2)

Centre frame

*Full-size plans of
greenhouse staging.*

Supporting
frames

Plan view

Plan view of lower shelf

3   Glue the outer two pieces of planking to the top of the frames, so that the two end frames are inset $^3/_{16}$in (4.8mm) from the ends, and fit the centre frame so that the tops of the uprights are exactly in the middle. The frames must be absolutely square with the planking, or the staging will not stand up properly. Add the other top planks, equally spaced between the two outer planks, and glue in place.

4   The lower planking can now be added: the two inner planks first, and then the four shorter outer planks. If the material used for the uprights is not exactly to the size listed, the four outer planks will have to be trimmed 'to fit'.

GROW-BAGS

If this is intended to be a modern setting, make grow-bags from pieces of Stay-soft dried flower base, uncooked Fimo, or Plasticine, covered with yellow plastic from a supermarket carrier bag. They should be approximately 3 x $1^1/_4$ x $^3/_8$in (76 x 31.8 x 9.5mm).

BORDER BED

If this is not to be a modern setting, or you don't want to have grow-bags, then you could make a greenhouse border bed by cutting a piece of balsa wood to fit from the rear to the front of the greenhouse, inside the base. Stain this for the edging board, and fix inside the base area to one side of the doorway. Then cut a piece of Oasis to fit in the space, and paint this soil colour.

GRAVEL FLOOR

Apply a coat of PVA glue to the exposed floor area inside the greenhouse base and cover it with railway layout ballast or birdcage grit for gravel. Birdseed such as Trill actually looks very convincing, but, living in the country, I have found that incorporating seeds in any kind of dolls' house project is not a good idea, and would be an open invitation for a greenhouse to become a mouse house!

GRAPEVINE

The grapevine growing up the far end of the greenhouse and under the roof was made from brown-covered sugarcraft wires and paper leaves, with grapes made from seed beads. It is easiest to fix the vine to the greenhouse framework before it is positioned on the base, unless you like working in very tight corners!

1   Cut a number of leaves of various sizes, to the shape given opposite, and glue them at intervals along a number of 24-gauge covered wires of varying length. Bunch the bottoms of the wire stems together and bind tightly with brown florists' tape. Glue the base of the bound stems into the far corner of the greenhouse so that the stems and leaves are against the end wall and partway across the underside of the roof apex.

The grapevine.

2   The bunches of grapes hanging from the vine in the roof are tiny glass seed beads. Thread about 15 or 20 beads onto a piece of 33-gauge covered wire, and twist the two ends of wire together, forming a loop to hold the beads loosely. Then twist the loop of beads around itself so that the beads form the shape of a bunch of grapes – the sort of thing that fine bead necklaces manage to do all by themselves when you don't want them to! Make a number of bunches in a similar way, with varying numbers of beads. The bunches can be sprayed with dark bluish-purple or very light green paint if your beads are not the right colour. Then they can be attached to the vine by twisting the free ends of wire around the stem and cutting off the surplus neatly.

Vine leaf pattern.

FINAL ASSEMBLY

Position the staging inside the greenhouse base about ¹/₂in (12.7mm) in from the edge and set the greenhouse on the base. I left the door in an open position, but you should be able to slide it to any position you want.

Do not glue the greenhouse to the base, so that it can be lifted off to make it easier to add things, move the contents around, and change the arrangement as desired.

GREENHOUSE PLANTS

Aquarium greenery, trimmed to shape where necessary, was used as the basis for the tomato, aubergine, and pepper plants.

TOMATOES

Fimo is my material of choice for these. I find that what is labelled 'transparent' or 'translucent' Fimo is very useful to mix with coloured Fimo and gives a more realistic colour for fruit and vegetables. Mix the suggested colours together until the resulting colour suits the vegetable you are making, and the Fimo is nicely softened. You can speed up the softening process a bit by warming the Fimo: I put it on top of a central heating radiator in winter. Conversely, if it gets too soft with being handled, put it in a cool place for a while.

Tomato plants. Mix ripe and unripe fruit for a realistic effect.

When using Fimo, work on a
spare piece of board covered
with foil. This stops the Fimo
sticking too much, and also stops
it picking up too much
discoloration from your hands.

Start with some red and a little transparent Fimo. You will also need a little yellow for not-too-ripe tomatoes and transparent and green for tomatoes which are definitely not ripe. Soften and roll the red and transparent Fimo together. Roll some of this into a sausage about $^{3}/_{16}$in (4.8mm) diameter and chop it up into bits about the same size. Add some yellow Fimo to part of the remaining red mixture to give it a more orange colour, and repeat. Then do the same again with more yellow added. Roll the bits into ball shapes in the palm of your hand and make a slight indent in the tops of the balls with the pointed end of a kebab skewer. Make some smaller unripe tomatoes in the same way, using transparent and green Fimo mixed together.

AUBERGINES (EGGPLANTS)

Use purple, a little black, and translucent Fimo. Make a sausage of $^{1}/_{4}$in (6.4mm) diameter and chop into $^{5}/_{8}$in (15.9mm) pieces. Shape the pieces to a slight taper with rounded ends.

PEPPERS

Use the same colours of Fimo as for tomatoes. Roll a sausage of $^{1}/_{4}$in (6.4mm) diameter, chop into pieces about the same size, and roll to give a tapered shape like a pepper. Use modelling tools to indent the sides and top.

Cook the Fimo tomatoes, peppers, and aubergines according to the manufacturer's instructions and stick them to the aquarium plants. There is a special Fimo adhesive which seems to work best for this.

*Pepper and aubergine
(eggplant), with a box of
picked fruit.*

PLANTING

Plant the tomatoes, peppers, and aubergines by pushing the base of the aquarium greenery into the Fimo or Oasis inside the grow bags. For an earlier period just plant tomatoes etc. in the greenhouse border bed, or in pots, as shown in the picture. Split bamboo kebab skewers lengthways for the plant stakes, and fasten the plant by sticking the plastic aquarium greenery to the stakes, or by tying them on with bits of fawn crochet cotton for raffia.

COLLECTED TOMATO, PEPPER, AND AUBERGINE

For picked fruit, a few finishing touches improve the effect. For tomatoes, paint a tiny dab in the indent with a very pale yellowy green, and add minute bits of greenery stuck into the indent of a few. For collected peppers, add a tiny bit of dried-plant stalk glued into the indent at the top of each pepper. Finishing touches can be added to collected aubergines by cutting a tiny circle of green paper napkin for each one. Stick one tightly, squashing as necessary, over the narrow end of each aubergine, and paint a tiny light-brown dot in the centre of the paper when the glue has dried.

Adding stalks to some of the tomatoes improves the effect.

PLANT POTS

Bought pots can be used for the large plants, but for small ones it may be necessary to make them by hand to get a realistic scale size. Make pots from Das, or similar, terracotta-coloured air-drying clay. I used part of a 'dolly' peg to shape the small plant pots. Cut the knob off a dolly peg and cover the cut end and the tapering part with clingfilm or Vaseline to stop the clay from sticking. Roll a small piece of clay out very thinly.

Cut a piece of rolled-out clay about 1½in (38.1mm) long and wrap the covered end of the dolly peg in it. Hold the peg vertically on the board and press down to flatten the bottom of the Das; then smooth the outside of the pot with a wet finger. Cut off the surplus clay at the top edge to give a pot about ½in (12.7mm) deep, by running a craft knife round the dolly peg. Leave to dry for a while, and when the clay starts to harden (you can tell because the colour becomes lighter), carefully turn the peg to keep it loose – otherwise it may be difficult to remove once the clay dries fully, as it contracts slightly during drying. When the clay is fully hardened, remove the peg. Don't worry too much if the top edge chips a bit when you remove the dolly peg former – many full-size clay pots have chipped edges, they aren't all perfect.

Larger pots can be made in the same way, using whatever comes to hand of the right shape and size as a former. When all else fails, I have used plastic covers from aerosol nozzles, plastic bleach-bottle tops, etc. as formers. Alternatively, use bottle tops of various sizes painted with terracotta Sandtex sample paint, or a similar colour of acrylic paint, for pots to hold greenhouse plants.

If you break some of your pots, they will look all the more authentic! The larger ones here are bought, the smaller ones handmade.

It is a good idea to use an old straight-sided glass bottle to do the rolling, and to work on a piece of kitchen foil or a clingfilm-covered board – otherwise you will be left with a messy area to clean up.

A few examples of easily made flowering plants which could be included in the greenhouse.

Suitable flowering plants can easily be made from bits of aquarium greenery with paper or thread flowers, using the information given in earlier chapters. Plant them into the pots with air-drying clay or Dri-Hard flower base. After the clay is dry, apply PVA glue to the exposed top surface and add medium-brown railway layout ballast or scatter material for potting compost. I used begonias (see page 40) and geraniums (see page 46). Smaller sprawling plants were made by gluing reindeer moss in the tops of the pots and then sticking coloured artificial stamens into the moss, as detailed on page 30. When the plants are complete, arrange the pots of flowers on the staging and use Blu-Tack or double-sided tape to hold the pots in position. It is handy to be able to lift the greenhouse to gain access.

WOODEN PLANT BOXES AND SEED TRAYS

Seed trays and seed packets.

1 Use thin balsa wood to make wooden plant and seed boxes to the plans provided. These drawings are only suggestions, as these boxes vary greatly, both in size and construction. They are often wooden trays which originally held fruit or vegetables and come from the local greengrocer's. To make plastic seed boxes of similar size, roll out some Fimo very thinly and use small blocks of wood covered in plastic film as formers: then bake according to the manufacturer's recommendations.

2 Leave some seed boxes empty, and part-fill some with Oasis, painted with dirty brown-coloured acrylic paint. Alternatively, simulate potting compost by coating the top surface with PVA glue and pressing fine dark brown railway layout ballast onto the surface.

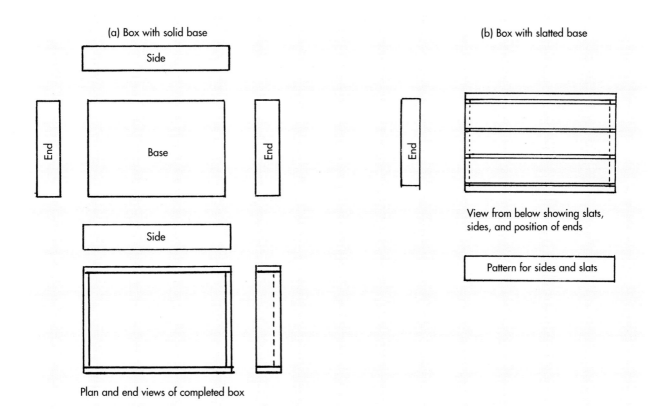

(a) Box with solid base

Side

End

Base

End

Side

Plan and end views of completed box

(b) Box with slatted base

End

View from below showing slats, sides, and position of ends

Pattern for sides and slats

3   For planted seed boxes, glue tiny bits of aquarium greenery or reindeer moss into holes in the Oasis. Individual bits of coloured foam scatter can be glued on some with tacky glue, for tiny flowers. Place a variety of boxes on and under the staging, leaving some for outside the greenhouse.

Full-size plans of wooden seed boxes.

CHRYSANTHEMUMS

Make a selection of chrysanthemum flowers in various colours. The ones shown in the photograph have leaves cut from paper and glued to the stems (see page 55 for the pattern). I used crochet cotton for the incurved ones, and shaded embroidery thread for the reflex ones (see page 55). They are fairly large, about ¹/₂in (12.7mm) across, as they are supposed to be potential prizewinners!

The chrysanthemums can either be planted directly into the Oasis bed, or planted into pots and the pots pushed into the flowerbed. I'm told that they are often grown in this way, because it makes it easier to bring the plants into the greenhouse to overwinter. Add a 4in (102mm) long piece of thin bamboo kebab skewer beside each plant for a stake, fastening the plants to them with dabs of tacky glue and/or fawn crochet cotton for raffia.

The prize chrysanthemums; the yellow flowers are of the incurved type.

SMALL GARDEN TOOLS

Thin sheet metal, from an empty drinks can, was used for the tools shown here, but you could use thin plastic sheet. Mark the shapes on the sheet from the drawing, and cut them out. Scissors should suffice for cutting either material, but don't use your best ones. Handles will be needed for the tools, cut from the relevant materials as detailed on the drawing. Attach the handle to the plastic or sheet metal tool by wrapping the handle part of the tool around the bottom of the handle, and gluing it in place. Superglue, or better still Ultrabond, is very good for this, but must be handled very carefully. For natural handles, just give them a coat of acrylic varnish, or use wood stain to colour them. Then paint part of the metal with Humbrol gloss paint as shown in the photograph.

Small fork and trowels.

Full-size patterns for hand tools.

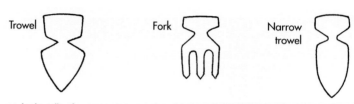

Make handles from ⅛in (3.2mm) dowel, ⅞in (22.2mm) long.

MODERN LAWN MOWER

1   A reasonable hover mower can be made very simply from an empty plastic tablet container (mine was an Anadin bottle). **Make sure that it is washed out thoroughly and allowed to dry, so that there is no residue of medicinal powder on it.** Cut around it to match the photograph, and make the two holes in the sides just below the cap. It looks best if you sand off the name from the top of the cap. Use Humbrol, or similar, model paint to paint the bottle part orange and the cap brown.

2   Bend a piece of white plastic-covered wire (Plastruct make this) to the shape given in the drawing, and push the ends into the holes; then bend them back on themselves inside the base, so that they can't pull out again. A second piece is glued on as shown to make the handle. If you don't have any Plastruct covered wire, use plastic-covered garden wire and paint it white.

MODERN WHEELBARROW

1   Cut thin metal, from an empty drinks can, or fairly stiff but thin card, to the pattern given. Score lightly along the fold lines, and fold up the shape. For sticking the metal use superglue, or Ultrabond, very carefully. From a strip of metal or card about ¼in (6.4mm) wide, cut short pieces to cover each corner of the wheelbarrow body. Fold these in half

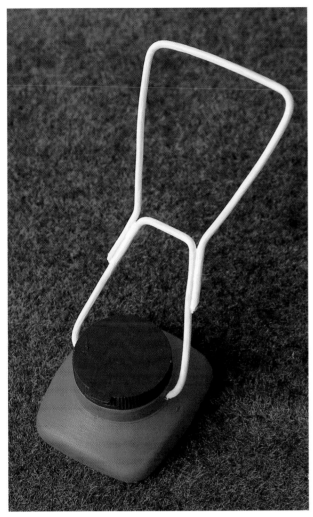

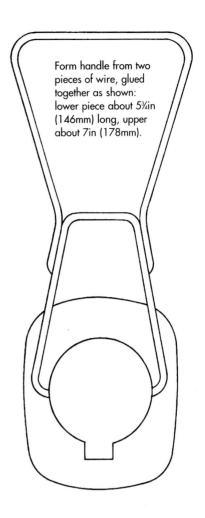

Form handle from two pieces of wire, glued together as shown: lower piece about 5¾in (146mm) long, upper about 7in (178mm).

The top of a plastic tablet container forms the basis of a convincing hover mower.

Full-size plan for hover mower. Shape of handle may have to be adjusted to suit the container available.

lengthways and stick one over each corner to keep the body in shape. When the glue has dried, give the whole thing a coat of paint – I used Plasti-kote aluminium spray paint.

2 The wheelbarrow framework aims to simulate tubular metal, so I used fairly thick, green plastic-covered garden wire. Use pliers to help bend the wire to the shape shown in the drawing. A short piece of red insulation from thick electric wire was used for handgrips, pushed over the ends of the garden-wire frame. An alternative would be red electricians' insulating tape, wrapped around the ends of the handles. Use a short piece, about ½in (12.7mm), of the plastic-covered wire as an axle, and push this through the hole in the centre of the wheel. You may have to enlarge the hole slightly to do this.

The metal wheelbarrow.

3 Assemble the wheel first, positioning the axle under the framework in the position shown in the drawing, so that the framework rests on top of the axle. Glue the axle in place with an all-purpose glue. When the glue has dried completely, glue the wheelbarrow body to the framework, as shown in the drawing and the photograph. The wheelbarrow could be used to hold and display collected vegetables from the greenhouse.

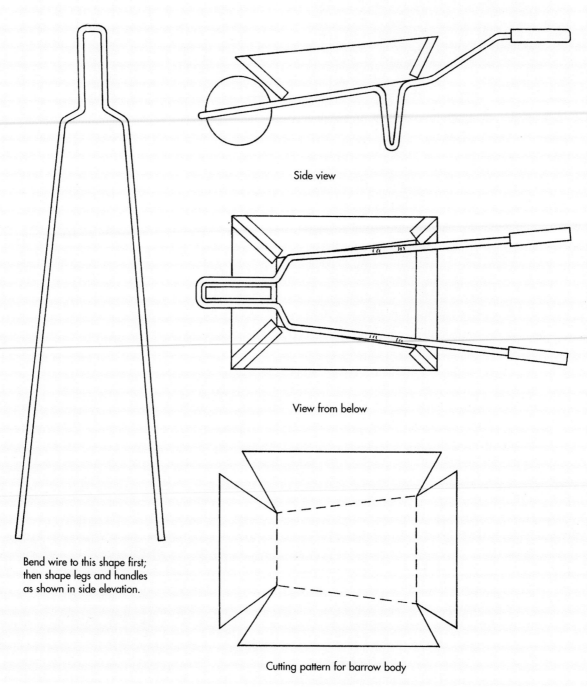

Side view

View from below

Bend wire to this shape first;
then shape legs and handles
as shown in side elevation.

Cutting pattern for barrow body

Full-size plans for metal wheelbarrow.

PLANK SEAT

1 Make a simple plank seat from two bits of thick twig for supports, about ⅝in (15.9mm) diameter, with a plank of balsa wood ⅛in (3.2mm) thick for the seat. You will need two fairly straight sections of twig 1½in (38.1mm) long, keeping the two cuts as square to each other as possible. Cut a piece of balsa wood 5in (127mm) long and 1in (25mm) wide and sand a slightly wavy shape to the edges to approximate a plank sawn straight from a tree. Colour the balsa plank with wood stain – I used light oak for the main part and a darker shade on the edges.

2 Set the twig sections upright, with 2½in (63.5mm) between them. Use PVA glue to fix the balsa plank across these. Position the plank seat on the grass mat and mark around the supports. Cut carefully on the line and scrape away the grass fibres from the area which will be covered by the seat supports, then glue the seat to the baseboard. Bits of green foam railway layout material can be stuck on with tacky glue to disguise any bits where the grass has been removed by mistake.

FURTHER ACCESSORIES

Coloured adverts for potting compost can be converted into bags of potting compost for the greenhouse. Cut out the adverts and glue to a chunk of Oasis or balsa wood of a suitable size and shape with PVA glue; then wrap the whole lot in clear self-adhesive plastic film (Fablon). Coloured adverts, or small parts of them, can be used for seed packets, chemicals, etc. Cut them out and glue them to suitable bits of Oasis or card, then cover them with clear plastic as above. If you want water available for your greenhouse, then borrow the hosepipe from the next project (pages 152 and 167).

A plank seat is one of the simplest garden accessories.

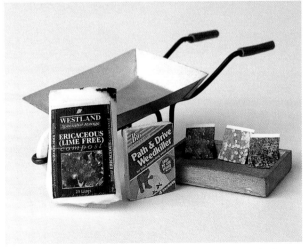

Bags and packets of garden products are easily made from magazine advertisements.

CHAPTER 15

KITCHEN GARDEN

This area of garden certainly provides plenty to do, keeping everything neat and tidy, and collecting fresh fruit and vegetables in the wheelbarrow for the kitchen. The project includes detailed instructions for making vegetables and fruit, both growing and harvested, from Fimo, paper, and aquarium greenery, and also features a fruit tree.

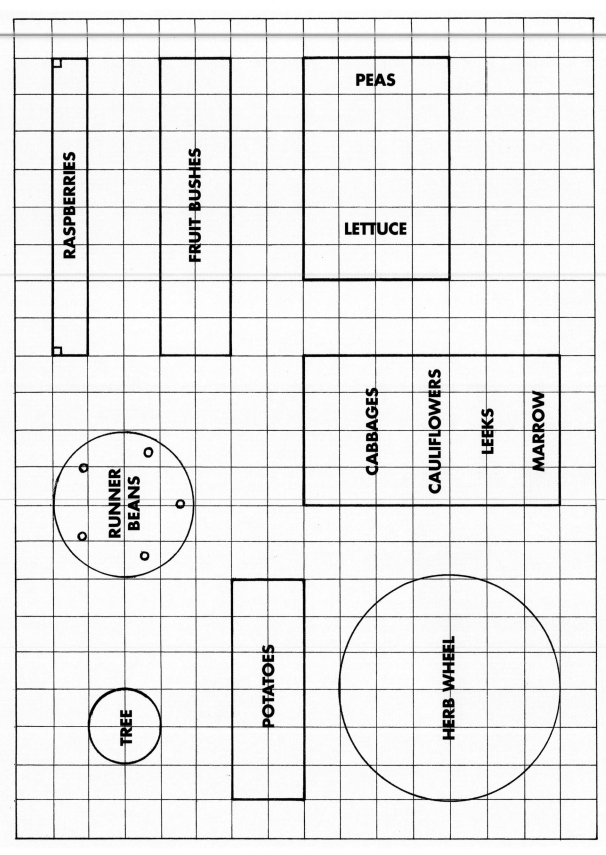

Ground plan of the Kitchen Garden.

- ❀ Baseboard: 9mm (³/₈in) MDF, 22 x 16in (559 x 406mm)
- ❀ Oasis rectangular blocks
- ❀ Grass mat
- ❀ Artificial greenery
- ❀ Fimo
- ❀ Balsa wood
- ❀ Paint
- ❀ PVA glue
- ❀ Bamboo skewers
- ❀ Paper napkins
- ❀ Tissue paper
- ❀ Dried flower material
- ❀ Thin sheet metal or plastic sheet
- ❀ Kebab skewers
- ❀ Twig
- ❀ Aquarium greenery
- ❀ Cocktail sticks
- ❀ Plastic-coated garden wire
- ❀ Railway layout flock material
- ❀ Sugarcraft covered wire
- ❀ Gravel or small stones
- ❀ Tile cement

BASEBOARD

Cut the MDF to the specified size and transfer an enlarged plan to the baseboard as detailed on pages 24–6.

VEGETABLE BEDS

Oasis rectangular blocks are used for the beds in which the vegetables grow. Cut into slices about ¹/₂ or ⁵/₈in (12.7 or 15.9mm) thick and then trim to fit the areas marked on the baseboard for fruit and vegetables. Glue them in place with PVA glue and leave to dry. When dry, round the edges off a bit and shape the top surface to take the planted vegetables as shown in the photographs.

HERB WHEEL

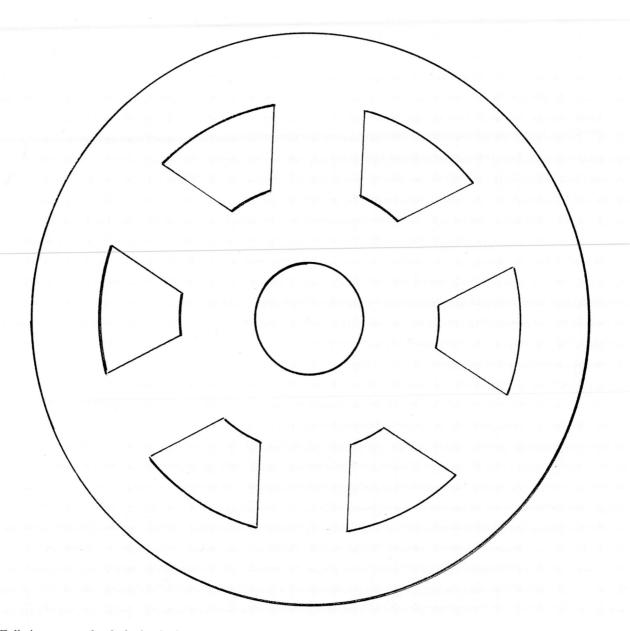

A bird's-eye view of the herb wheel.

1 Transfer the herb wheel pattern to the baseboard. For the cobbles I used fish tank gravel – a bag of small rounded gravel cost me very little. Apply a thin layer of tile cement to the cobbled area, a little at a time, and press individual pieces of gravel into the cement to fit as neatly as possible over the area. When you have covered all the cobbled area, leave until the tile cement is completely set.

2 For the herbs themselves, reindeer moss in various shades seemed the obvious answer. Glue this to the baseboard with PVA glue, in clumps between the cobbled areas, using a different shade of moss for each area.

Full-size pattern for the herb wheel.

GRASS

Cover the remaining area of the baseboard with grass mat stuck down with PVA glue. Carry the grass mat over the edges of the baseboard as for the Cottage Garden (see page 116), and either leave the edges as they are or add wooden edging over the grass mat (see page 23 and photo on page 60).

TREE

1   For this tree I used sea lavender. Select some nicely branched pieces and bunch them together to form a satisfactory tree shape about 8in (203mm) high. Spray the flowery branched parts green. I used Plasti-kote leaf-green spray paint **(remember the safety recommendations on page 11)**. When the paint is dry, apply PVA glue to the lower stems, before the branching starts, and bind them all tightly together with brown florists' stem tape to form a tree trunk.

The fruit tree, with apple-picking in progress.

2   Set the bottom end of the tree in air-drying clay to form a good base. A piece about the size of a golf ball should be enough. Press the clay onto a board and push the base of the trunk into the centre of it, then spread the clay out from the trunk, tapering down to the board, so that the base spreads out fairly widely and somewhat irregularly to approximate the tops of tree roots. This will give your tree a firm support. When the clay has dried, paint it to blend in with the tree trunk, and leave for the paint to dry. Fix the tree firmly to the baseboard in the same way as for the tree in the Cottage Garden (see page 121). You will need to support it until the glue sets.

3   If you want a fruit tree, make the fruit as detailed below. Use Fimo glue to fix them to the undersides of the branches close to the leaves. Don't put too much on, or the branches will be weighed down.

FRUIT BUSHES

1   These are also made from sea lavender. Select a number of suitable pieces between 3in (76mm) and 4in (102mm) long, and spray the flowery bits green, as for the tree, but preferably a different shade of green. When the paint is dry, bunch two or three bits together to form a nice bush shape, apply PVA glue to the bottom 1in (25mm) or so of the stems, and bind them together tightly with brown florists' tape around the plain bits at the base. Plant the bushes in the Oasis bed marked for them on the plan, using PVA glue to hold them in place.

Fruit bushes and raspberry canes.

2   Stick bits of red foam scatter beneath the leaves with PVA glue for redcurrants. For gooseberries use seed beads or yellow or green foam scatter, and stick these on similarly.

A selection of garden tools. The small border spade is made to a slightly reduced version of the spade pattern given in the drawings.

RASPBERRIES

Make a support frame for raspberry canes from two pieces of $^1/_4$in (6.4mm) square wood 5in (127mm) long, and lengths of stiff florists' wire. Glue the pieces of wood upright on the baseboard in their marked positions and cut four pieces of stiff florists' wire slightly longer than the gap between the posts. Make holes in the posts about 1in (25mm) apart and glue the ends of the florists' wire into them between the two posts. Use a number of brown covered wires 6in (152mm) or 7in (178mm) long for the raspberry canes and coat with green flock material as detailed on page 32. Alternatively, use long thin pieces of sea lavender, sprayed green.

Bunch together the bases of the stems in groups of two or three, bind the bottom bits tightly together, and plant in the Oasis alongside the support frame. Spread the canes against the support wires and add individual bits of red flock for raspberries.

Full-size patterns for garden tools.

GARDEN TOOLS

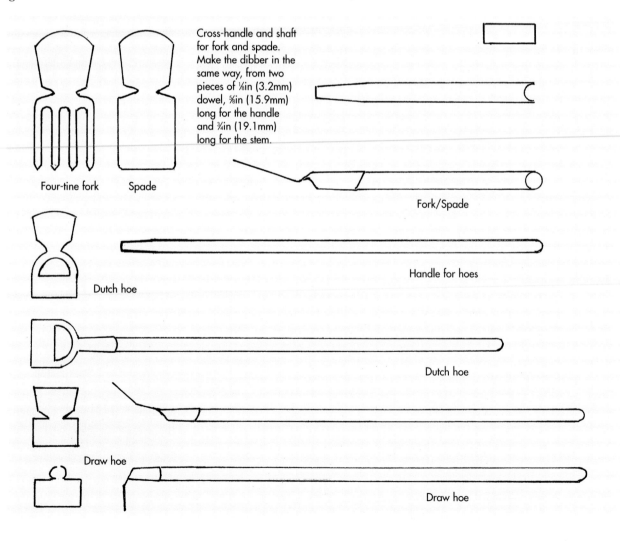

Cross-handle and shaft for fork and spade. Make the dibber in the same way, from two pieces of ⅛in (3.2mm) dowel, ⅝in (15.9mm) long for the handle and ¾in (19.1mm) long for the stem.

Four-tine fork   Spade

Fork/Spade

Dutch hoe

Handle for hoes

Dutch hoe

Draw hoe

Draw hoe

These are larger than those used in the previous chapter for the greenhouse, but are made in a similar way out of thin sheet metal from an empty drinks can, or thin plastic sheet, cut to the plans provided. Cut handles from kebab skewers or dowelling and either give them a coat of acrylic varnish or paint them with model paints. Attach the relevant handles to the tools as for the greenhouse tools in the previous chapter, using Ultrabond or superglue very carefully according to the manufacturer's instructions.

WOODEN WHEELBARROW

Cut pieces of balsa wood to the patterns given in the drawings. Harder wood will give a better result, if you have the equipment to cut it. Sand each piece gently for a good fit. If you wish to stain the wheelbarrow, now is the time to do it. Assemble the body of the wheelbarrow as shown in the drawing.

A disc of balsa serves for the wheel. Fix this in place by pushing a cocktail stick through the holes in the side supports and the wheel as shown. Apply glue to the outside of the wheel and axle, then trim the cocktail stick to length with a sharp craft knife. If you intend to paint your wheelbarrow, use a proprietary grain filler and sanding sealer, before sanding lightly and painting.

The traditional wooden wheelbarrow.

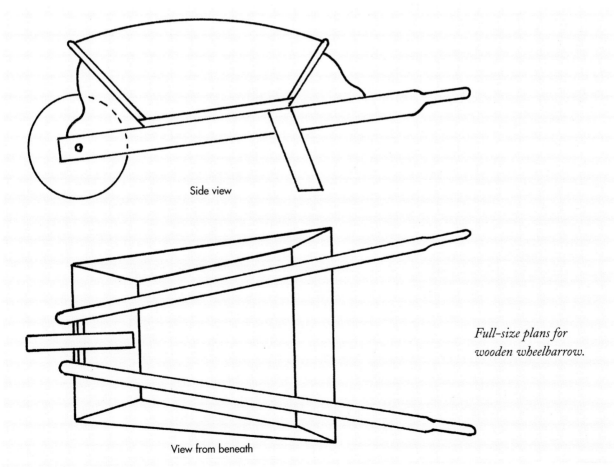

Side view

View from beneath

Full-size plans for wooden wheelbarrow.

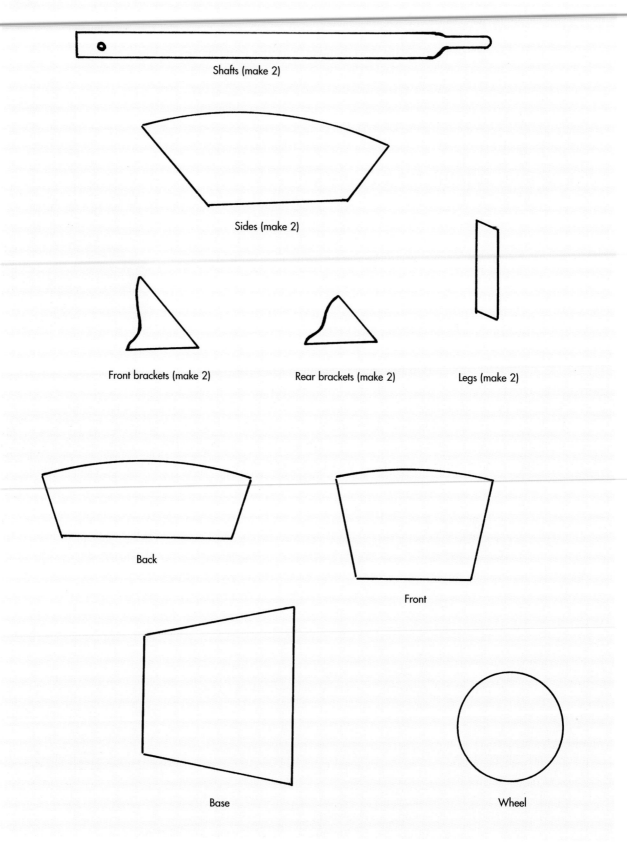

Shafts (make 2)

Sides (make 2)

Front brackets (make 2)   Rear brackets (make 2)   Legs (make 2)

Back

Front

Base

Wheel

Full-size patterns for wooden wheelbarrow.

PICKED VEGETABLES

Various colours of Fimo were used to make fruit and vegetables as shown in the photographs. Patterns for some of the vegetables are given below.

Make a few of each of the larger fruit and vegetables, and rather more of the smaller ones, of your choice, to put in the wheelbarrow. Remember that if you want to turn your tree into a fruit tree you will need extra of whichever fruit you have chosen to use.

RUNNER BEANS

I used green, white, translucent, and a touch of yellow Fimo. Flatten the mixed and softened Fimo, on a piece of kitchen foil, into a very thin layer. Slice this into strips, some about $^1/_2$in (12.7mm) and some $^5/_8$in (15.9mm) wide. Then use a craft knife to cut across the strips at about $^1/_{16}$in (1.6mm) intervals. The cuts don't need to be exactly straight as, thank goodness, beans don't grow perfectly straight!

Runner beans.

PEAS

Green, white, and transparent Fimo can be used to make a suitable colour for peas. After mixing together, roll small bits into a sort of long, thin sausage about $^1/_{16}$in (1.6mm) in diameter. Use a not-too-sharp implement to cut this into tiny bits about $^1/_4$in (6.4mm) long, or a little bit more for some. This should give a suitable pinched end to each piece, like a pea pod.

CARROTS

Orange Fimo used on its own, I find, looks too artificial. I add some white and transparent to the orange. Roll a $^1/_8$in (3.2mm) diameter sausage and chop it up into different-sized bits, from $^1/_4$in (6.4mm) to $^3/_8$in (9.5mm) long, then roll one end of each piece against the board so that the typical tapered carrot shape is formed. Make an indent in the top (wide) end with a cocktail stick. When the carrots have been baked hard and cooled completely, add the finishing touches. Carrots look more realistic with a tiny bit of fine ferny aquarium plant stuck into the indent in the top. Larger carrots benefit from a few very fine marks round them, at intervals: I use light brown acrylic paint and a very fine paint brush.

Peas and carrots.

SPROUTS

Tiny balls of Fimo left over from the beans can be used, and marks made over the surface with a modelling knife for the leaves, but I prefer to use tissue paper, although it is a sticky, fiddly, and messy job.

Tear small bits of green tissue paper, about 1in (25mm) in diameter, and roll up very tightly. This I find is best done by crumpling it up first, and

Cauliflowers (in the barrow), cabbages, lettuces, sprouts.

Full-size patterns for vegetables.

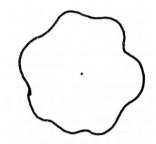

Cabbage leaves

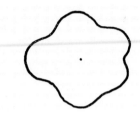

Lettuce leaves

Cauliflower leaves

then using the fingers (or one finger) of one hand to roll the ball of paper in the palm of the other hand. (In just the same way, many years ago, pharmacists made hand-rolled pills). Finished sprouts should be no larger than about $\frac{1}{8}$in (3.2mm). Finally, coat with matt spray varnish. I put the sprouts in a foil dish, hold the dish in one hand, and jiggle it about to keep the sprouts on the move, while I operate the spray with the other hand. Then I tip the sprouts onto a piece of foil to dry.

CABBAGE

A similar method is used to make the heart of the cabbage. Use a darker green paper and start with a larger piece, so that you end up with a ball about $\frac{3}{8}$in (9.5mm) to $\frac{1}{2}$in (12.7mm) in diameter. For a stalk, cut a piece about 1in (25mm) long from the point end of a cocktail stick. Coat the pointed bit with PVA glue and push into the cabbage heart to glue it in place. For outer leaves cut three or four more pieces of the same paper to the pattern. Crumple these up and then partially straighten them out again; this sounds like a waste of effort but gives the effect of crinkly leaves. Apply a dab of tacky glue to the bottom of the cabbage heart, around the stalk, push a crumpled piece over the stalk, and stick it to the base of the cabbage heart. Repeat for the other leaves. Arrange the leaves to your satisfaction and spray with matt varnish to fix them in place.

LETTUCE

These are made in exactly the same way as the cabbages, only with lighter green tissue paper, a smaller heart, and leaves cut to the lettuce pattern given opposite.

CAULIFLOWER

Again the same method is used as for the cabbage. Cauliflowers need white paper for the heart or flower part and leaves cut to the cauliflower pattern opposite from bluey-green tissue or napkins.

LEEKS

White and transparent Fimo form the basis for a good leek. Roll a sausage about $\frac{3}{16}$in (4.8mm) diameter and chop into pieces about $\frac{3}{4}$in (19.1mm) long. These need to be baked, before the leaves can be stuck on.

Green tissue or paper napkin about 1in (25mm) square is used to form the leaves for the leeks. Make narrowly spaced cuts, about $\frac{1}{8}$in (3.2mm) apart, along one side, cutting to halfway across the square. Apply PVA glue to the uncut part, and wrap around the white Fimo leek, overlapping the white by about $\frac{1}{4}$in (6.4mm).

POTATOES

Mix light brown, white, and a little transparent Fimo together and form irregularly shaped oval-to-round pieces about ¹/₈in (3.2mm) to ¹/₄in (6.4mm) in size. Place on the tray to bake with the other vegetables. The photograph shows a pail full of collected potatoes. Instructions for making the pail are given on pages 166–7.

Potatoes.

PLUMS

Fimo in purple, red, yellow, and transparent is used for these. Mix to the colour you want – this is one time when unevenly mixed colours can be an advantage. Roll a sausage about ¹/₈in (3.2mm) diameter, chop it up into bits about ³/₁₆in (4.8mm) long. Roll these into egg shapes, then use a modelling tool to put an indent in one end, and continue with a slight crease mark on one side, from one end of the oval to the other. When the plums have been baked hard and cooled completely, add the finishing touches. On one or two stick a tiny bit of dried grass stem into the indent on the top for a stalk. Add a small pointed oval leaf cut from an old silk leaf or paper to a few of the ones with stalks.

Plums.

APPLES, ROSY DESSERT TYPE

Mix some red and transparent Fimo together, and some yellow and transparent. Roll a sausage of the red mixture, about ¹/₄in (6.4mm) diameter, and a sausage of the yellow mixture about ¹/₈in (3.2mm) diameter. Lay these alongside each other, pressed together but not mixed. Roll to form a ¹/₄in (6.4mm) diameter sausage. The rolling should give a sort of marbled effect to the sausage. Chop the sausage into pieces about ³/₁₆in (4.8mm) long, and roll each into a ball. Use something like a wooden kebab skewer to make a fairly large indent at one end for the top, and a smaller indent at the opposite end for the bottom.

APPLES, GRANNY SMITH OR GOLDEN DELICIOUS TYPE

Several kinds of apples: Granny Smiths in the box, other varieties in foreground.

For Granny Smith or Golden Delicious-type dessert apples use green and transparent Fimo, with a tiny bit of yellow for Granny Smith type and more yellow for the Golden Delicious type. Soften and mix the colours together. Roll to form a ¹/₄in (6.4mm) diameter sausage, then make the apples as above.

BAKING APPLES

Baking apples can be made in the same way as rosy dessert apples, by mixing green Fimo with the yellow mixture and making the marbled sausage a bit thicker, to give bigger apples.

FINISHING TOUCHES

When the apples have been baked hard and cooled completely, add the finishing touches. Apply a dab of brown paint to the indent on the bottom. On one or two, stick a bit of dried flower stem into the indent on the top for a stalk, and add an oval leaf cut from an old silk leaf, paper, or aquarium greenery to a few of the ones with stalks.

GROWING VEGETABLES

The growing vegetables shown are mostly formed from aquarium plastic plants or paper.

RUNNER BEANS

The runner beans on their canes.

Runner bean leaf

1   Use thin bamboo skewers for canes. Stick five canes into the Oasis as shown in the main drawing and tie the tops together firmly with buttonhole thread or covered wire. Add a touch of tacky glue to keep the thread securely fastened. Select aquarium plant mat with oval or heart-shaped leaves about ³/₈in (9.5mm) long and ¹/₄in (6.4mm) wide, and secure to the bamboo canes. Alternatively, cut a number of leaves to the shape given opposite, but varying the size of some of them. Wind green-covered wires loosely around each cane for the bean stems, then put a dab of tacky glue on each leaf in turn, and stick them to the covered wires.

2   Red foam flock material is used for the flowers of the runner beans. Cut short bits of fine, green-covered wire, coat about ¹/₂in (12.7mm) of one end with tacky glue, and press this into a small heap of red foam flock. Push the other end of the wire in a block of Oasis until the glue dries. Repeat until you have enough flowering stems for your bean plants. When the glue is dry, trim each wire in turn to a suitable length for the position you want to put it in, and glue it to the bean stalk with PVA glue, to create runner beans in full flower as shown in the photograph.

3   Use some of the beans made as described on page 161. Glue them to short pieces of green-covered wire, preferably in small groups of two or three, then glue the wire to the plant so that some beans can be seen hanging down.

CABBAGES AND CAULIFLOWERS

Make six or seven cabbages as detailed on page 162. Stick them to the Oasis with tacky glue in their allotted space. To indicate where cabbages have been removed for use, apply tacky glue to a small area of the Oasis vegetable bed and dig into it with a kebab skewer to make a hole with a small mound of Oasis

earth around it. Colour to match the surrounding bed once the glue has dried. Cauliflowers, made as detailed on page 162, can be planted in the same way.

The central vegetable plot, with marrow or courgette (zucchini) plant, leeks, cauliflowers, and cabbages.

SPROUTS

When they are growing it is not always easy to see the sprouts too well, and they would be very small until fairly late in the year anyway. Use the smaller version of the plan for cauliflower leaves and form a sort of rosette, as if for a flower, glued on the end of half a cocktail stick. Spray with hairspray or varnish to stiffen the leaves, and when dry paint the stick a very light green. Add a few lower leaves by pushing the cocktail stick through the centre and gluing the leaves to the stalk at intervals. If you want to add sprouts, stick them around the cocktail-stick stalk, beneath the top rosette of leaves, and between the lower leaves. Plant the sprout stalks in a row as for the cabbages.

LEEKS

The only part you see when they are growing is the leaves, so use a short piece of bamboo skewer instead of the leek bulb and make leaves to attach to the top as on page 162. Stick these into the Oasis in a straight line.

MARROW PLANT

Use a piece of aquarium greenery, suitably trimmed down to size, for leaves of a marrow plant, and trail it across the front row of the vegetable bed in front of the leeks. Make a yellow paper flower (a pattern is given opposite), and form as if for a large floret (see page 36). Stick the flower on the greenery.

Marrow flower

POTATOES

These need to be planted in the top of a ridge. Aquarium plant mat with small leaves can be chopped into bits and stuck into the Oasis in rows, as all you would see is the potato tops or leaves.

PEAS

Use cocktail sticks, minus their points, for supports, and fine (33-gauge) green covered wire for garden string, to form a pea support frame. Select aquarium mat greenery with small leaves for the plants, and stick the stems into the Oasis in a row, then push the cocktail sticks into the Oasis and add the garden string for the pea supports. A few Fimo pea pods left over from the collected vegetables (see page 161) can be stuck on to hang down from the greenery.

CARROTS

The right-hand plot, with peas and lettuce. The dibber and line are ready for planting out seedlings.

All that is seen of growing carrots is their tops, so a line of fine feathery aquarium green will suffice, positioned in the vegetable bed as shown. If you use a short piece of green covered wire and attach the feathery green to this, it will help to keep the carrot tops more upright, as will a coat of spray varnish.

LETTUCE

The photograph shows a few lettuce remaining in the patch, so make some lettuces as given for collected vegetables (see page 162) and stick them to the Oasis in rows of uneven length; indicate the removal of some, in the same way as for the cabbages. Seedling lettuce can be made from a circle of green tissue, about 1/2in (12.7mm) diameter. Use a short bit of fairly thick covered wire and push this through the centre of the circle. Add PVA glue and stick the paper to the wire, squeezed up a bit to look like a plantlet.

LADDER

The ladder is made from wood strips and cocktail sticks. Cut two pieces of strip wood and make holes in both pieces, as indicated. Cut cocktail sticks to the length shown and glue them into the holes to form the rungs. Coat with either matt acrylic varnish or acrylic paint. Rest the ladder against the tree ready for fruit-picking time.

Real metal pails can be made from drinks cans – the right-hand one has yet to be painted!

PAIL

Cut thin drinks-can metal to the pattern shown. Roll into a cone shape and glue together very carefully with a drop of superglue or Ultrabond on the overlap flap shown.

As it is very small, I recommend that you handle this with tweezers to make sure that you don't glue your fingers to it.

Cut a circle of balsa for the base. Glue the snipped edge and push the balsa into the cone to form a base a little up from the bottom of the pail. Paint the pail aluminium colour when the glue has dried.

Bend the handle to shape from florists' iron wire, and attach in the same way as for the wooden bucket on page 125.

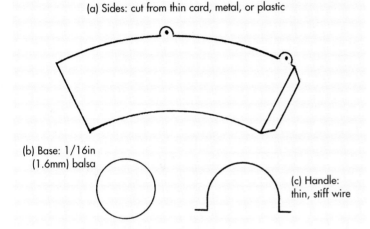

(a) Sides: cut from thin card, metal, or plastic

(b) Base: 1/16in
(1.6mm) balsa

(c) Handle:
thin, stiff wire

Full-size patterns for the metal pail.

CUT FLOWERS

Make a selection of cut flowers to your choice from thread and/or tissue paper as detailed in earlier chapters. I would suggest daisy-type flowers (see page 58), larkspur (see page 49), dahlias (see page 55), and asters (see page 57). Alternatively, select suitable bits of dried plant material: tiny flowers, grasses, sea lavender, etc.

FINISHING TOUCHES

Position the wheelbarrow with collected fruit and vegetables displayed in it, and a pail of potatoes and/or cut flowers to your taste; perhaps stick the garden fork or spade into the Oasis soil of one of the vegetable beds ready for the next lot of digging. Add a hose from plastic-coated garden wire. Tidy up the garden area a little by gently blowing off any unwanted loose bits, but don't make it too tidy – it wouldn't be natural!

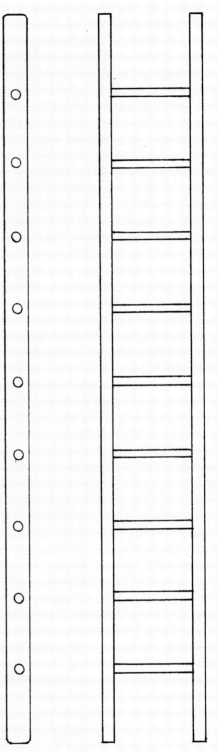

Full-size pattern for ladder.

CHAPTER 16

WINDOW BOXES

Now for something completely different. If space for displaying a miniature garden is limited, why not hang one on the wall? This project is more vertical than horizontal, being basically part of the front of a house, with the 'gardening' confined to window boxes, hanging basket, and pots.

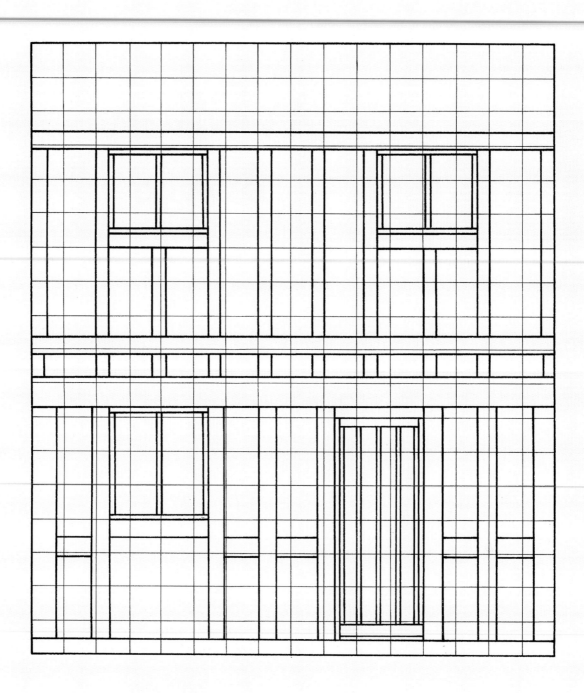

General layout of house front.

MATERIALS

- ❀ MDF: 9mm (³/₈in) thick for the base and the house wall, 4mm (⁵/₃₂in) thick for the roof
- ❀ Sweeping-brush head: a cheap one with brown bristles
- ❀ Dress net, black
- ❀ PVA glue
- ❀ Balsa wood, ¹/₁₆, ³/₃₂ and ¹/₄in (1.6, 2.4, 6.4mm) thick
- ❀ Household filler
- ❀ Paint and wood stain
- ❀ Clear acetate sheet, or similar
- ❀ Film drawing pen
- ❀ Flower materials
- ❀ Egg box
- ❀ Wood glue
- ❀ Small nails or panel pins
- ❀ Oasis
- ❀ Thick card
- ❀ Mirror brackets
- ❀ Small wood screws
- ❀ Doorknob

BASEBOARD

Cut a piece of 9mm (³/₈in) MDF 16 x 4in (406 x 102mm) for the baseboard.

HOUSE WALL

1   A piece of 9mm (³/₈in) MDF 16 x 18in (406 x 457mm) is needed for the house wall. Using something like Evo-Stik Resin W wood glue, attach the wall to the edge of the baseboard at exact right angles. Strengthen the joint by pinning with panel pins, or by drilling holes in the wall piece along the centre line of the thickness of the base and screwing in small screws tightly. Allow the glue to dry thoroughly before proceeding.

2   Enlarge the drawing on page 172 and transfer it to the MDF. (You might prefer to do this before attaching it to the baseboard; but remember to leave the space at the bottom where the base will be fitted.)

3   Cut balsa wood for the over-sail (protruding) beams to the pattern on page 173, stain them a fairly dark colour, and when the stain is dry glue them in position on the house wall as shown on the main drawing.

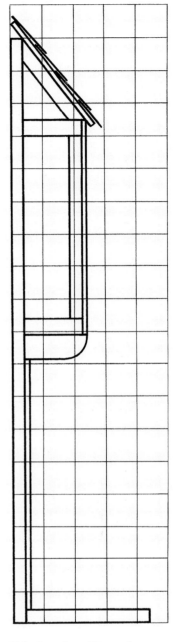

Side elevation of house front.

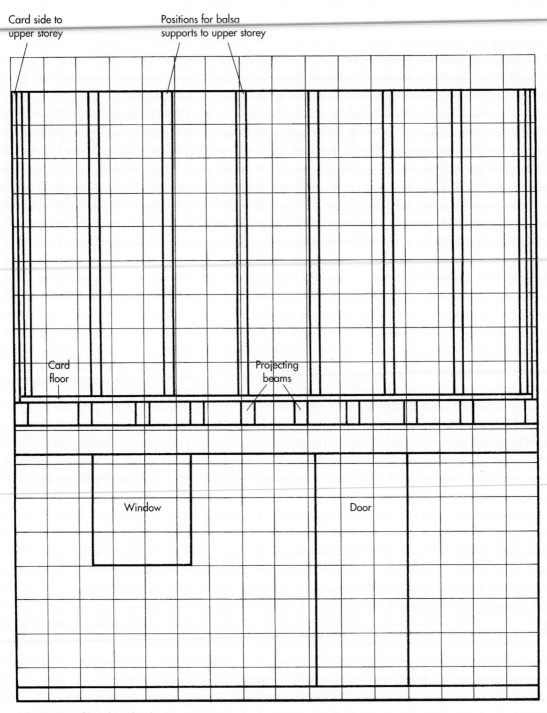

Card side to
upper storey

Positions for balsa
supports to upper storey

Card
floor

Projecting
beams

Window

Door

Position of baseboard with crazy paving

Pattern to be enlarged and transferred to the main 18 x 16in (457 x 406mm) board.

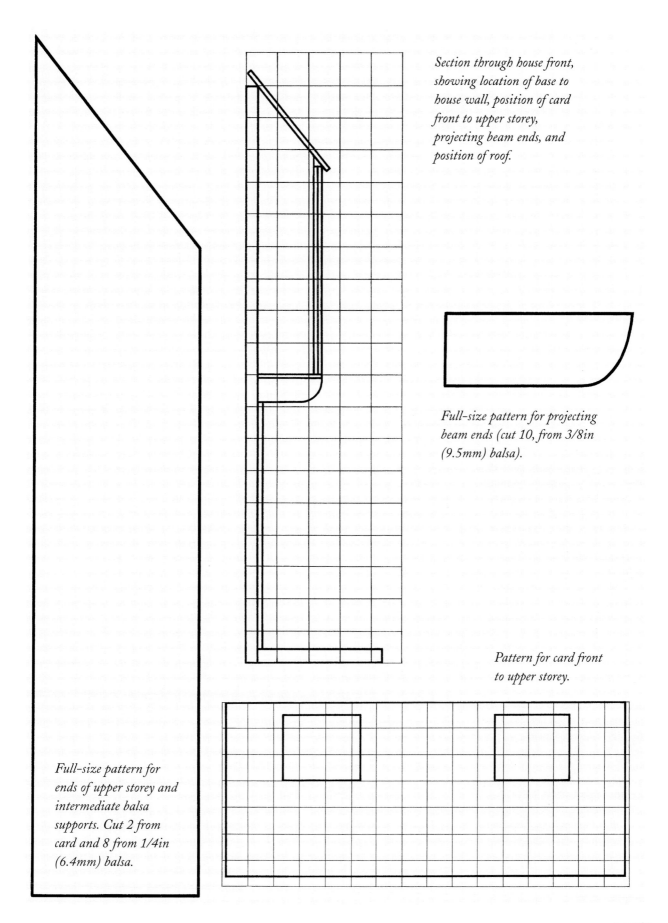

Section through house front, showing location of base to house wall, position of card front to upper storey, projecting beam ends, and position of roof.

Full-size pattern for projecting beam ends (cut 10, from 3/8in (9.5mm) balsa).

Pattern for card front to upper storey.

Full-size pattern for ends of upper storey and intermediate balsa supports. Cut 2 from card and 8 from 1/4in (6.4mm) balsa.

4   To save on weight, the upper house wall and sides are made of very thick card, cut to the patterns on page 173. The upper-storey flooring is also made from card, and should be cut 'to fit'; the sizes given on the drawing are theoretically correct, but may need altering a little depending on your actual construction. Balsa wood 1½ x ¼in (38.1 x 6.4mm) is used to support the upper house front, again for weight-saving. Cut eight pieces to the same size and shape as the pieces of card for the sides. Glue these firmly to the wall, one at each end, one each side of the two window areas, and one in the centre. When completely dry, glue the card house front, floor, and sides onto these supports, and hold firmly in place until the glue dries.

5   Colour-match pots of household emulsion (latex) paint were used for painting the house wall: a light ivory colour for the main areas, and a medium grey-blue for the window areas. Try not to obliterate the lines around the windows, as you will need to see these to fix the window framing.

6   For the timber, cut ³/₃₂in (2.4mm) thick balsa-wood strips to the widths given in the drawings for the lower and upper house walls. Cut the strips a bit longer than shown, so that you can trim them 'to fit'. It is easy to trim a bit off, but not easy to add a bit on! Stain them and allow to dry. When dry, glue them in place on the walls, trimming them to fit as you go.

WINDOWS

A close-up with the window box removed shows the details of the first-floor window and the texture of the thatched roof.

1   Cut sufficient balsa wood strips ¹/₁₆in (1.6mm) thick and ³/₁₆in (4.8mm) wide to fit around the window areas twice over, and stain them. When the stain has dried, glue one layer of strips around each window area.

2   Use clear acetate sheet to cut window glazing to size. With a film pen and ruler, draw diagonal lines onto the acetate sheet to approximate the pattern shown in the photograph. Make sure there are no finger marks on the window glazing sheet, position, drawn side inwards, over the window areas, and hold in place temporarily with tiny bits of double-sided tape. Now glue the second layer of already stained framing strip around each window, sandwiching the glazing between this and the first layer.

DOOR

The front door and the rambling rose.

Cut ¹/₁₆in (1.6mm) balsa wood for the door, and from the same thickness cut facing strips as shown in the drawing. Cut door frame strips from ³/₃₂in (2.4mm) balsa wood, stain them, and when the stain is dry glue the pieces together to form the integral door and door frame as shown on the drawing. Finally, glue the whole door assembly in position on the lower house front and hold firmly in place until the glue has set.

ROOF

1 Cut 4mm ($^5/_{32}$in) MDF to size for the roof base. This measures $16^1/_4$ x $3^5/_8$in (409.6 x 92.1mm).

2 Draw lines horizontally across the roof base, about 1in (25mm) apart. Glue a layer of brush bristle along the lowest line with PVA glue, overlapping the MDF at the side edges; brush more PVA onto the top portion of the bristles as necessary to get them to stick well. Then add another layer of bristles across the next line up in the same way. Repeat this procedure until all but the topmost part of the roof has been covered. For this last part, glue the bristles on so that they overlap the top of the roof base. When the whole of the thatch has thoroughly dried, trim the bristles to your satisfaction, so that they protrude about $^3/_8$in (9.5mm) below the roof base, and only slightly above the top edge of the roof.

3 Black dress net was used for sparrow netting. Cut this about 2in (51mm) larger than the roof thatch all the way round and glue in place, applying the glue to the underside of the MDF and pressing the net firmly onto this. Pull the net firmly, but not *too* tightly, over the thatch. You may find it easier to use a piece of double-sided tape on the underside of the roof base and press the net onto this: then, when you are happy with the result, secure the edges of the net with glue.

4 If you wish to hang this project on a wall, now is the time to fix two mirror brackets onto the back with small screws.

5 Now glue the roof in place on top of the upper storey wall and the back piece of MDF, making sure that it is held firmly in place until completely dry.

CRAZY PAVING

1 Spread an even layer of interior household filler, such as Polyfilla or Unifilla, mixed to a fairly stiff paste, over the baseboard area as shown on the plan. Be careful not to get any filler on the house wall, door, and timbering. Spare bits of clear acetate can be used to shield these if necessary.

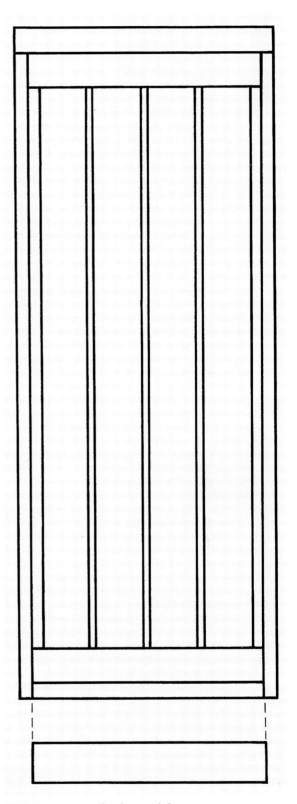

Full-size patterns for door and doorstep.

A bird's-eye view of the crazy paving.

2 Mark out the main area for crazy paving using a sharp tool of some kind, such as an awl. When dry, smooth if necessary with wet-and-dry paper.

3 Remove any sanding dust with a damp cloth before painting. I used a coat of beige household emulsion paint to start with. After this was dry a thin wash of brown, green, and ochre watercolour paint was used to give varying shades to the paving. The spaces between the paving were coloured with sepia watercolour, and the whole area given a couple of coats of matt acrylic varnish to seal the surface.

4 Final trimming was done with tiny bits of green foam scatter material glued on with tacky glue, as for the steps in the Walled Garden project (see page 84).

RAMBLING ROSE

Cut a small bit of Oasis about ³⁄₈in (9.5mm) thick to fit the space left for a flowerbed to the right of the door, and glue firmly in place. I used long pieces of dried plant material with small leaves for the main plant part of the climbing rose. The bases of the stems are glued into the Oasis flowerbed, and the plant pushed back against the wall, held there by small dabs of tacky glue where necessary. Handmade paper roses (see page 41) and buds were then glued on to turn the climber into a reasonable representation of a rambling rose.

FLOWERBED

At the base of the climbing plant, clumps of reindeer moss were glued on and tiny bits of dried flowers stuck to this to finish it off.

WINDOW BOXES

1 Cut strips of ³⁄₃₂in (2.4mm) balsa wood to the sizes given. You will need one set for each window box. Stain all the pieces, and when the stain is dry glue them together to form window boxes as shown on the drawing and in the photograph.

Base
(cut 3)

Front and
back (cut 6)

Ends (cut 6)

Full-size patterns for window boxes.

The colourfully planted window boxes.

2 When the glue has dried, cut Oasis or dryfoam to fit inside each window box and glue it in place with tacky glue. Make flowers of your choice, or select suitable dry

plant material for the planting. The ones shown in the photograph were mostly handmade: trailing geraniums (see page 48), pelargoniums (pages 46–7), and petunias (page 51).

TERRACOTTA-STYLE TUBS AND POTS

1   Satisfactory terracotta tubs were made by cutting up a compressed-card egg carton. With a sharp craft knife, cut round just above where the egg usually sits, at a level to avoid too much of the adjoining bits of the carton.

2   Paint the outside with terracotta exterior household paint, such as Sandtex, from a sample tin. Pots made this way would look equally effective painted with stone-coloured Sandtex.

The egg-carton pots each have a geranium in the centre.

3   To add weight and keep the pots from being easily tipped over they need to be filled with something heavy such as air-drying clay; I used Stay-Soft, which is made for flower arranging and is usually available from florists. As the name suggests, it doesn't go hard, so plants and flowers can easily be pushed into it.

4   To plant the pots shown in the photographs I used handmade flowers, dried plant material, and reindeer moss. For the centre I chose a relatively large geranium with handmade leaves (see page 47); I made red flowers for one pot and pale pink ones for the other. The stems are simply pushed into the Stay-Soft. Pieces of green reindeer moss were glued around the central geranium and draped over the edges of the pots. A large number of different pansy flowers (see page 53) were stuck to the reindeer moss, keeping groups of one type together. Small coloured stamens were also stuck into the reindeer moss for smaller flowers. The final shaping was created by short pieces of light greyish-coloured dried flower material stuck in, for a plant such as helichrysum, and tiny bits of feathery green aquarium plant added in the gaps.

The other pot plants could be any of those described in earlier chapters.

HANGING BASKET

1   Another section of egg carton was used to make a hanging basket. This was cut and painted as for the tubs, but this time filled with Oasis, which was glued inside, because it needs to be fairly light.

2   To suspend the hanging basket I used button thread. Make evenly spaced holes around the edge with a large darning needle, tie a short length of buttonhole thread to each hole, and secure with a dab of tacky glue.

The hanging basket features trailing geraniums and petunias.

The besom.

After planting the basket, gather together the ends of thread and tie tightly together, so that the basket hangs level. Secure the knot with PVA glue, and trim the ends of the thread.

3　The basket shown was planted with trailing geraniums (see page 48), petunias (page 51), and straggly bits of reindeer moss hung over the sides.

BESOM

For the handle cut a piece of wooden kebab skewer about 3in (76mm) long. A bundle of sweeping brush bristles is used for the broom head, bunched around the lower end of the handle and bound tightly with buttonhole thread. This should be knotted neatly, and the whole binding secured with a coat of tacky glue.

FIXING WINDOW BOXES AND HANGING BASKET

1　Give all the planted window boxes, pots, tubs, etc., a covering spray with matt varnish such as Crystal Clear acrylic spray, remembering the safety rules for using sprays, and allow to dry thoroughly. This will help to protect the paper flowers from discolouration and dampness, and will make dust removal easier.

2　Glue the window boxes in place beneath each window, as shown in the photographs. When the glue has dried, use tweezers to arrange the trailing plants gently.

3　For the hanging basket, make a small hole in one of the protruding beams and push a short piece of brown covered wire through it. Twist the wire ends tightly together beneath the beam for about ¹/₂in (12.7mm), cut through the wire, and bend the cut end upwards to hold the hanging basket. Alternatively, if there is a tiny gap, you can just hang the basket by slipping the knotted threads over a beam, as I have done.

FINISHING TOUCHES

Arrange the planted terracotta pots, tub and pot plants on the crazy paving, and hold them in place with a tiny bit of Blu-Tack. If you are hanging the project on your wall and want to fasten the pots permanently, use PVA glue. Finally, position the besom broom against the wall at the side of the door, and again, hold in position with either Blu-Tack or PVA glue.

CHAPTER 17

FURTHER USES FOR MINIATURE GARDEN IDEAS

I suggested in Chapter 1 that parts of model garden projects, or adaptations of garden ideas, could be used for making attractive gifts. A few possibilities are included here.

For a quick, small, personalized gift, or as a feature for outside a dolls' house, egg-carton pots can be made as detailed in the previous chapter (page 177) and quickly filled with simple plantings made from reindeer moss with either small bits of dried flower material or handmade paper flowers.

The well in the Cottage Garden project could also be used by itself. Follow the instructions for making the well, as given on pages 121–5. Cut a 5in (127mm) diameter circle of very thick card or 4mm ($^5/_{32}$in) MDF for the baseboard. Glue the well to this, and then glue grass mat and reindeer-moss plants around the base. A circle of craft felt glued to the underside of the base will finish it off nicely.

A selection of egg-carton planters.

Different parts of the egg carton can be used to make tall planters or bird baths.

Alternatively, make just the well base as given in the instructions on page 123. Make flowers of your choice from paper, thread, or reindeer moss, or collect together some small silk flowers, dried plant material, and reindeer moss of various colours. Fill the centre of the well with Dri-Hard or air-drying clay, and arrange your flowers and plants, pushing the stems firmly into the clay. When the clay has dried, finish off by gluing bits of reindeer moss on, to cover the exposed bits of clay and drape over the edge of the well base. Again, craft felt can be glued to the bottom with advantage.

A further alternative is to cut a small round block of Oasis in half to give two half-height planters. These could be marked out for brickwork, as above, or for stone, as shown in the photograph.

A well base used as a planter.

Two square brick beds.

Low stone planters.

Raised beds in brick and stone.

As an inexpensive present for a friend who is interested in dolls' houses, a small raised brick bed can be made quite quickly. Styrofoam comes in other shapes and sizes than those used previously in this book. There is a small square block, about 3in (76mm) square. Mark this out for brickwork, as shown for the large raised bed on page 91, paint it, and plant the top to suit your taste – or better, the taste of the person for whom you are making it. As a change from the basic red brick, one of those shown was painted with a light tan-coloured matt acrylic paint, with odd patches of a darker shade. The planting uses only bought silk flowers, dried flower material, aquarium greenery, and reindeer moss; it can therefore be made quickly. This would be ideal for a gift to a friend or relative, but the dolls' house enthusiast would probably be 'over the moon' with a similar one planted with handmade scale-size flowers.

Square planters can also be made half-height by cutting the block through the middle. These are very effective when marked out and painted to simulate various kinds of stone. If you have offcuts of larger Oasis blocks left over, these can be used for small planters or raised beds, marked out for either brick or stone and painted a suitable colour.

For a small dolls' house garden, cut a piece of board to the required size and use the plants detailed in earlier chapters to create your own flower scheme. Even a piece only 6 x 4in (152 x 102mm) can make a beautiful rockery or flower border to sit in front of a dolls' house. Rockeries look very effective, made with either bits of real slate or small pebbles stuck together with tile cement and surrounded by grass mat. The small border shown here is created on a piece of board 8 x 4½in (203 x 114.3mm).

A small rockery made of real slate.

Two mini-rockeries, one of slate, one of pebbles.

A small herbacious border makes a fine miniature garden in its own right.

Small ponds can be created like that shown below. This was made using one layer of plasterboard and finished in a similar way to the one given in the Pond and Rockery project (see page 105).

If either you or a friend are interested in making and/or collecting miniature pot plants, why not make a greenhouse to house them? That way they would be largely protected from dust, but you could still see them; and the display could develop into something quite spectacular. Make, and glaze, a greenhouse as shown on pages 134–9. Cut a piece of board just a little larger than the greenhouse – say 9 x 7in (229 x 178mm). Add a gravel floor, and cover the outside edges with grass mat material, wrapping it over the edges of the baseboard as described on page 116. Make wooden staging for one side (see pages 140–2) and arrange your pots on the floor and staging.

Another very nice present for a gardener would be a wooden wheelbarrow planted with either bought silk flowers and dried plant material, or handmade paper flowers. Make a wheelbarrow as given on pages 159–60, and glue Oasis inside to hold the flowers. Then plant it with your choice of materials, and spray with matt varnish to hold the flowers in shape and help with dust removal. Cut a small piece of MDF or plywood, cover the top with railway layout grass material and the base with felt. Fix the planted wheelbarrow in position on this. The ideal would be to have a clear plastic cover to go over the top.

You can, of course, combine individual elements from any of the projects. You could put the well next to the patio, instead of the raised bed, and have a wooden bench seat to sit on. Add a rustic chair to the walled garden, or a plank seat to the pond and rockery. In the kitchen garden you could change or add to the vegetables planted in the beds, add a hover mower to cut the grass, or have a modern wheelbarrow instead of the wooden one.

There are endless possibilities, and enormous pleasure to be had from experimenting with different arrangements. Many of the ideas given here could be used as alternatives in your own garden projects. I hope that you have as much fun with your miniature gardens and get as much pleasure from them as I do.

The miniature pond is constructed just like the larger one in Chapter 12.

The greenhouse by itself can be used to display a colourful collection of flowers.

CONVERSION TABLES

FRACTIONS OF AN INCH

In $^1/_{32}$in increments, with the metric equivalents correct to one decimal place.

in	mm	in	mm	in	mm	in	mm
$^1/_{32}$	0.8	$^9/_{32}$	7.1	$^{17}/_{32}$	13.5	$^{25}/_{32}$	19.8
$^1/_{16}$	1.6	$^5/_{16}$	7.9	$^9/_{16}$	14.3	$^{13}/_{16}$	20.6
$^3/_{32}$	2.4	$^{11}/_{32}$	8.7	$^{19}/_{32}$	15.1	$^{27}/_{32}$	21.4
$^1/_8$	3.2	$^3/_8$	9.5	$^5/_8$	15.9	$^7/_8$	22.2
$^5/_{32}$	4.0	$^{13}/_{32}$	10.3	$^{21}/_{32}$	16.7	$^{29}/_{32}$	23.0
$^3/_{16}$	4.8	$^7/_{16}$	11.1	$^{11}/_{16}$	17.5	$^{15}/_{16}$	23.8
$^7/_{32}$	5.6	$^{15}/_{32}$	11.9	$^{23}/_{32}$	18.3	$^{31}/_{32}$	24.6
$^1/_4$	6.4	$^1/_2$	12.7	$^3/_4$	19.1	1	25.4

INCHES PLUS FRACTIONS

Metric equivalents are corrected to one decimal place.

	0	1	2	3	4	5	6	7	8	9	10
0		25.4	50.8	76.2	101.6	127.0	152.4	177.8	203.2	228.6	254.0
$^1/_{16}$	1.6	27.0	52.4	77.8	103.2	128.6	154.0	179.4	204.8	230.2	255.6
$^1/_8$	3.2	28.6	54.0	79.4	104.8	130.2	155.6	181.0	206.4	231.8	257.2
$^3/_{16}$	4.8	30.2	55.6	81.0	106.4	131.8	157.2	182.6	208.0	233.4	258.8
$^1/_4$	6.4	31.8	57.2	82.6	108.0	133.4	158.8	184.2	209.6	235.0	260.4
$^5/_{16}$	7.9	33.3	58.7	84.1	109.5	134.9	160.3	185.7	211.1	236.5	261.9
$^3/_8$	9.5	34.9	60.3	85.7	111.1	136.5	161.9	187.3	212.7	238.1	263.5
$^7/_{16}$	11.1	36.5	61.9	87.3	112.7	138.1	163.5	188.9	214.3	239.7	265.1
$^1/_2$	12.7	38.1	63.5	88.9	114.3	139.7	165.1	190.5	215.9	241.3	266.7
$^9/_{16}$	14.3	39.7	65.1	90.5	115.9	141.3	166.7	192.1	217.5	242.9	268.3
$^5/_8$	15.9	41.3	66.7	92.1	117.5	142.9	168.3	193.7	219.1	244.5	269.9
$^{11}/_{16}$	17.5	42.9	68.3	93.7	119.1	144.5	169.9	195.3	220.7	246.1	271.5
$^3/_4$	19.1	44.5	69.9	95.3	120.7	146.1	171.5	196.9	222.3	247.7	273.1
$^{13}/_{16}$	20.6	46.0	71.4	96.8	122.2	147.6	173.0	198.4	223.8	249.2	274.6
$^7/_8$	22.2	47.6	73.0	98.4	123.8	149.2	174.6	200.0	225.4	250.8	276.2
$^{15}/_{16}$	23.8	49.2	74.6	100.0	125.4	150.8	176.2	201.6	227.0	252.4	277.8

INDEX

abrasives 21
adhesives 9
air-drying clay 12
apples 163–4
aquarium plants (greenery) 16, 31, 37
artificial stamens 15, 30
asters 57
aubergines 144, 145

baseboards 23
begonias 40
besom 178
brick raised beds 90, 91–3, 180–1
bridge, rustic 108–10
brushes 11
buds 36
bucket/pail 125–6, 166–7
bulrushes 107
bush roses 41, 42
bushes 31–2
butterfly 129

cabbages 161, 162, 164
camellias 41, 97
carnations 56
carrots 161, 166
cauliflowers 161, 162, 165
chairs/seats
    garden seat 69–72
    patio chair 98–101
    plank seat 151
    rustic chair 128–9
chrysanthemums 54–5, 147
circle and stamen method 33–5, 40–6
clamps 21
climbing rose 67–8
cocktail sticks 22
conversion tables 183
Cottage Garden 112–29
craft knives 18–19
crazy paving 175–6
cut flowers 167

dahlias 55–6
daisy-like flowers 58
delphiniums 48–9
dished circles 34
'do-it-yourself' (DIY) products 8–9
door 174–5
double begonias 40
double flowers 34
drawings 6–7
dried flowers 13
drills 21

edges, neatening 23
edging plants 68
egg-carton planters 177, 179
eggplants 144, 145
enlarging plans 24–5, 26
equipment 17–22

fabric leaves 38
fading 36
fence 116–21
files 20
Fimo 11, 38, 143–4
fixatives 14
flag iris 52, 106, 107
flock material 16, 31, 32
floret method 35–6, 46–51
floribunda roses 41, 42–3
flower-making techniques 33–8
    specific flowers 39–58
foam flock material 16, 31, 32
fruit, picked 163–4
fruit bushes 157

garden seat 69–72
garden tools 148, 158–9
gate 119–20
geraniums 46–8
grapevine 142–3
grass materials 12
grasses 13
gravel floor 142
greenhouse 133–9, 182
    staging 140–2
Greenhouse Garden 130–51

greenhouse plants 143–5
grow-bags 142

halved joints 64–5
hand garden tools 148
hanging basket 177, 178
hedgerow twigs 16, 32
herb wheel 156
herbacious border 181
hollyhocks 43–4
house wall 170, 171–4
hybrid tea rose 42

iris, flag 52, 106, 107
ivy-leafed geraniums 48

Kitchen Garden 152–67
knives, craft 18–19

ladder 166, 167
larkspur 49
lawn mower 148, 149
leaves 37–8
leeks 162, 165
lettuce 161, 162, 166
lighting 18

magnifiers 18
mallow plant 126–7
marking out 18
marrow plant 165
materials 6, 8–16, 29
measurements 6–7
measuring 18
metric equivalents 7, 183
mitre block 19, 23, 24
model railway materials 16, 32
modelling tools 19

nasturtium 49–50
neatening edges 23
needles 22

Oasis 12, 34, 77
odds and ends 16
ornamental poppy 45–6

pail/bucket 125–6, 166–7
paints 10, 11
pampas grass 98
pansies 53
paper 14
paper flowers 33–6, 40–53
  circle and stamen method
    33–5, 40–6
  floret method 35–6, 46–51
paper leaves 38
patio chair 98–101
Patio Garden 86–101
paving 63, 89–90, 134, 175–6
peas 161, 166
pelargoniums, zonal 46–7
peppers 144, 145
petunias 51
picked fruit and vegetables 144,
  145, 161–4
pins 22
plaited trimming 100–1
plank seat 151
plans 24–6
  enlarging 24–5, 26
  transferring 24
plant boxes 140, 146–7
plant pots 145
planters 95–6, 177, 179–80
Plastruct 133, 134
pliers 20
plums 163
polymer clay 11, 38, 143–4
pond plants 107–8
Pond and Rockery Garden 102–11
ponds 105–6, 182
  surface 108
poppy, ornamental 45–6
pot plants 31, 97–8, 146, 182
potatoes 163, 166
pots, plant 145
  see also planters
potting compost 151
pump 85
punches 20–1

railway layout materials 16, 32
raised beds 90, 91–3, 180–1
rambling rose 43, 176
raspberries 157, 158
razor saw 18–19, 24
reed mace 107
reeds 107
reindeer moss 15, 30–1
rockeries 107, 111, 181
rockery plants 29–30
roof 174, 175
roses 41–3
  climbing 67–8
runner beans 161, 164
rustic bridge 108–10
rustic chair 128–9

safety 59
scale 4, 6
scissors 20
sea lavender 13, 30
seats see chairs/seats
seed boxes 140, 146–7
seed packets 151
silk flowers 14
simple plants 29–32
single flowers 34
sink garden 96–7
spray booth 27–8
spraying 11
sprouts 161–2, 165
squaring jig 27
staging 140–2
staining 70
stamens, artificial 15, 30
statice 13, 30
stem tape 15
steps 84
stream 105–6, 108
styrofoam block 12, 34, 77
styrofoam trays 21, 35
sugarcraft tools 20

terraced beds 82
terracotta planters 95–6, 177
thread 15
thread flowers 36–7, 54–8
timbering 174
tomatoes 143–4, 145
tools 17–22
  garden tools 148, 158–9
trailing geraniums 48
trees 117, 121, 157
trellis arch 64–7
Trellis Arch Garden 60–73
trug 73
tubs
  terracotta–style 177
  wooden 93–4
tweezers 19
twigs, hedgerow 16, 32

varnish 10
vegetables
  picked 144, 145, 161–4
  plants 143–5, 164–6

Walled Garden 74–85
walling 77–80
water lilies 108
well 121–6, 179–80
wheelbarrows
  modern (metal) 148–50
  wooden 159–61, 182
window boxes 176–7, 178
Window Boxes project 168–78
windows 174
wire 15
wire cutters 20
wood 8
wooden tub 93–4
working area 17

zonal pelargoniums 46–7